DINNER
IN A **DASH**

DINNER
IN A DASH

75 Fast-to-Table and Full-of-Flavor
DASH Diet Recipes from the Instant Pot®
or Other Electric Pressure Cooker

HARVARD
COMMON
PRESS

Nancy S.
Hughes

Brimming with creative inspiration, how-to projects, and useful information to enrich your everyday life, Quarto Knows is a favorite destination for those pursuing their interests and passions. Visit our site and dig deeper with our books into your area of interest: Quarto Creates, Quarto Cooks, Quarto Homes, Quarto Lives, Quarto Drives, Quarto Explores, Quarto Gifts, or Quarto Kids.

© 2019 Quarto Publishing Group USA Inc.
Text © 2019 Nancy S. Hughes
First Published in 2019 by The Harvard Common Press, an imprint of The Quarto Group,
100 Cummings Center, Suite 265-D, Beverly, MA 01915, USA.
T (978) 282-9590 F (978) 283-2742 QuartoKnows.com

The Harvard Common Press titles are also available at discount for retail, wholesale, promotional, and bulk purchase. For details, contact the Special Sales Manager by email at specialsales@quarto.com or by mail at The Quarto Group, Attn: Special Sales Manager, 100 Cummings Center, Suite 265-D, Beverly, MA 01915, USA.

23 22 21 20 19   1 2 3 4 5

ISBN: 978-1-55832-959-1

Digital edition published in 2019
eISBN: 978-1-55832-960-7

Library of Congress Cataloging-in-Publication Data

Names: Hughes, Nancy S., author.
Title: Dinner in a dash : 75 fast-to-table and full-of-flavor dash diet
   recipes from the instant pot or other electric pressure cooker / Nancy S.
   Hughes.
Description: Beverly, MA, USA : Harvard Common Press, 2019. | Includes index.
Identifiers: LCCN 2018057875 | ISBN 9781558329591 (trade pbk.)
Subjects: LCSH: Pressure cooking. | One-dish meals. | LCGFT: Cookbooks.
Classification: LCC TX840.P7 H84 2019 | DDC 641.5/87--dc23 LC record available at https://lccn.loc.
gov/2018057875

Design: The Quarto Group
Cover Photography: Maria Siriano
Page Layout: Megan Jones Design
Illustrations: Shutterstock

Printed in China

The information in this book is for educational purposes only. It is not intended to replace the advice of a physician or medical practitioner. Please see your health-care provider before beginning any new health program.

To my husband, Greg who's there . . . right there to offer support, a helping hand, a critique . . . even when I don't necessarily ask for it . . . but always with a smile!

To my "ever-expanding" family . . . Will, Kelly, Molly, Anna Flynn, Hootie, Terry, Annie, Jillian, Jesse, Emma, Lucy, Taft, Kara, River, and our Baby Girl on the way . . . whew! So many personalities, so many taste buds . . . so much fun!

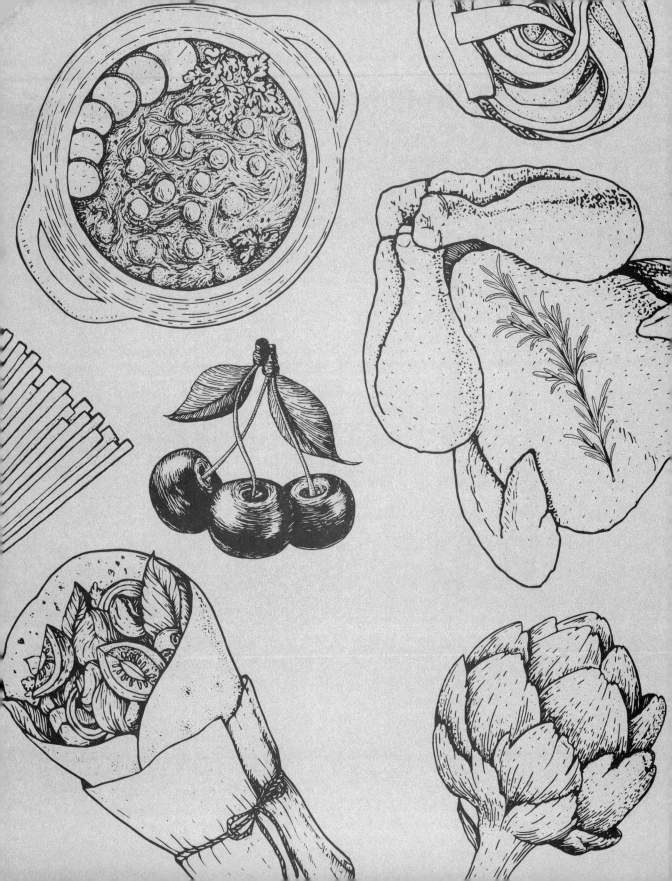

Contents

INTRODUCTION:
DASH Diet and Pressure Cooker Basics

What is the DASH Diet?

The letters "D-A-S-H" stand for Dietary Approaches to Stop Hypertension. Doctors strongly recommend the DASH Diet for people who have heart disease; they highly recommend it for people who are at risk for heart disease; and they just plain recommend it for anyone who doesn't ever want to get heart disease—which is just about everyone!

Recipes that adhere to the DASH Diet, which includes all of the recipes in this book, are created to help lower or control high blood pressure and cholesterol levels. They do this by emphasizing foods that are lower in sodium and rich in nutrients, such as potassium, magnesium, and calcium. Both high blood pressure and high cholesterol are major risk factors for heart disease.

Bring Down That Sodium a Little

Cutting back on your sodium intake does not mean sacrificing flavor, nor does it mean making more work for yourself by having to prepare more ingredients to replace that salt. What it *actually* means is that you are introducing a boatload of new flavors while letting the electric pressure cooker (*not you*) do the work! We all know that "no salt" or "low salt" recipes can be flavorless, but it doesn't have to be that way. By using readily available, "normal" ingredients found in your local grocery store and simple techniques with the pressure cooker, the flavors of your dish will intensify without overdoing the salt . . . you'll see!

The trick is also knowing *how* and *when* to add sodium to make it more pronounced, so you can use less sodium and it won't get hidden or lost during the cooking process.

Sodium control is very important. Most of us know that there's *tons* of sodium in processed foods. But do you also know that items you may think are healthy, like lite salad dressings, bottled salsas and spaghetti sauce, pouches of rice, canned veggies, pickles, and even ketchup, are loaded with sodium? Even those healthy-sounding canned soups, chicken and turkey lunch meats and sausages, meatless patties, and some frozen veggies with light sauces can be through the roof with sodium levels!

According to the DASH guidelines, the limit of sodium for a meal ranges from 500 mg to 700 mg, depending on which diet is chosen. My goal was to develop recipes that stayed around 500 mg of sodium per serving. So whether you have a sodium limit per meal of 500 mg or 700 mg, all of the recipes in this book are for you!

Pump Up Those Nutrients!

While taking control of your sodium intake, it's important to incorporate nutrient-rich ingredients into your dishes. This does not have to make you feel like you are being restricted; it is actually introducing new flavor profiles and new taste sensations.

One way to do this is to give those fruits and veggies more attention. Put them in the spotlight and include more in each dish to add vitamins, minerals, fiber, and color. How they're cut or roughly mashed can give character and texture to a dish. Give them some personality and you'll find that you have a lot of options you never considered before.

Foods high in potassium, magnesium, and calcium are particularly important. Some of the foods listed below provide more than one of these nutrients—an extra bonus in nutritional benefits, for sure. Every single recipe contains ingredients that are rich in potassium, magnesium, and/or calcium.

FOODS HIGH IN POTASSIUM

Potassium helps control your blood pressure. With the aid of your kidneys, potassium helps remove extra sodium from your body through your urine. Potassium helps the walls of your blood vessels relax or loosen up. When they're too tense or rigid, it can lead to high blood pressure, which can cause heart problems. Getting enough potassium is good for your heart.

You also need enough potassium for good muscle health, so that your muscles can flex and contract the way they should (don't forget that your heart is also a muscle!). And your nerves need potassium so that they can function properly. Foods that are high in potassium include the following:

- Dried fruits, such as apricots, dates, raisins, figs, and apples
- Wild-caught salmon, mahi-mahi, tuna, halibut, cod, and trout
- Beans, peas, and other legumes, especially large white beans, pinto beans, kidney beans, edamame, and lentils
- Avocado
- Potatoes (sweet and white)
- Acorn, butternut, and zucchini squash
- Spinach, Swiss chard, kale, and collard greens
- Cucumbers
- Eggplant
- Pumpkin
- Broccoli
- Low-fat yogurt, cream cheese, milk, and buttermilk
- Mushrooms (all varieties)
- Banana, kiwi, cantaloupe, pomegranate, and cherries

FOODS HIGH IN MAGNESIUM

Magnesium is an important mineral that your body needs in order to function. It produces energy and regulates blood sugar and chemical reactions in the body. Magnesium helps maintain the proper levels of other minerals, such as calcium, potassium, and zinc. Your heart, muscles, and kidneys all need magnesium to work properly. The mineral also helps build teeth and bones. Foods that are high in magnesium include the following:

- Dark leafy greens, such as spinach, Swiss chard, kale, turnip greens, and collard greens
- Seeds, especially sesame, flax, chia, pumpkin, hemp, and sunflower
- Lentils and beans, especially lima, navy, and black beans
- Whole grains, such as quinoa, whole wheat pasta, brown rice, barley, and wild rice
- Fish, such as mackerel, salmon, halibut, tuna, and cod
- Nuts, especially peanuts, almonds, cashews, pine nuts, walnuts, and pecans

- Dark chocolate: baking chocolate (100% cocoa) and dark chocolate (85% cocoa or more)
- Nonfat and low-fat yogurt, skim milk, and reduced-fat cheese
- Avocado
- Bananas
- Bran cereal

FOODS RICH IN CALCIUM

Calcium helps support bone health, may help prevent cancer, aids in weight management, and improves blood pressure and heart health. Calcium helps blood vessels tighten and relax when they need to. Foods that are high in calcium include the following:

- Low-fat yogurt, cheese, and skim milk
- Some leafy greens, especially collards, kale, turnip greens, and spinach
- Beans, especially white beans, edamame, peas, and lentils
- Clams and mussels
- Okra
- Salmon (especially canned salmon) and trout
- Acorn squash
- Seeds, such as sesame seeds
- Almonds
- Fortified breads, tortillas, and crackers
- Figs

Electric Pressure Cooking

Avoiding heavily processed prepared foods and making meals from scratch are the best ways to follow the DASH Diet. Does this mean you need to spend hours in the kitchen? No! Electric pressure cookers, including the Instant Pot and a host of models from other manufacturers, are a great tool for making nutritious and fresh home-cooked meals in a flash.

There are many reasons to own an electric pressure cooker, including the following:

1. It doesn't heat up the entire kitchen.
2. You don't have to closely monitor boiling pots.
3. All the cooking is done in one pot, so you only have one pot to wash.
4. It doesn't use a lot of energy.
5. Food cooks in a fraction of the time than on the stove top or in the oven.
6. It cooks tough cuts of meat quickly.
7. You can use it to brown ingredients initially.
8. It allows you to make healthy "comfort" meals effortlessly while filling the room with a heady aroma.
9. It helps you stay on a healthy track because you're not missing out on . . . anything!

What do you do with a pressure cooker when you're not using it? Leave it out on the counter as you would a coffee pot or small microwave, if possible. That way, it will be available and easily accessible. Or, store it so it's easy to reach in a cabinet or cupboard close by. Make a special spot for it; that way, you'll use it a lot more often— and cook healthier meals more often, too!

SIMPLE THINGS YOU MIGHT NEED

- Small food scale (very inexpensive)
- Ruler (to measure various cut sizes for accurate cooking times)
- Trivet (which usually is included with the pressure cooker)
- Collapsible steamer basket (to hold ingredients that would slip through the trivet)
- 8-inch (20 cm) nonstick springform pan (it will fit into 6-quart [5.7 L] and larger pressure cookers)

- 1½-quart (1.4 L) round oven-safe casserole dish or bowl
- Paper towels (to help add "traction" when removing skin from chicken pieces)

ELECTRIC PRESSURE COOKING TIPS

1. Take a timer with you if you plan to leave the kitchen. The timer and the pressure pin on the pressure cooker are relatively faint to hear and you may miss it . . . and mess up, too!
2. If you need to add ingredients after you've removed the lid from the pressure cooker, it may be difficult to lock the lid again. Simply wait a minute and try again. It may take a couple of tries, but it will lock into place.
3. If the lid doesn't lock into place, it could be that the plastic ring is not inserted into the lid all the way. Just press down all the way around, securing the ring in place, and then try again.
4. Cook with the pressure cooker in an open area. Do not place it under a shelf or hanging cabinet/cupboard. When the steam is released, it will "steam" your shelf or cabinet and may warp your shelving over time.
5. For the most part, the recipes in this book are developed to serve four. Occasionally, some of the recipes will serve six or more, but leftovers can be frozen for a later time.

This book was designed to make life deliciously easier and healthier, so you can take control of your sodium levels and increase your intake of "good-for-you" foods, and with the convenience of the pressure cooker, dinner will be ready in a dash! *Enjoy!*

1

Wraps, Sandwiches, and Tortillas

Power-Packed Greek Pitas

4 ounces (115 g) dried brown lentils, rinsed

4 cloves garlic, peeled

1 dried bay leaf

2 cups (475 ml) water

2 ounces (55 g) kale, chard, and spinach
   mix, coarsely chopped

1 cup (135 g) chopped cucumber

¼ cup (40 g) chopped red onion

2 ounces (55 g) pepperoncini, sliced

3 ounces (85 g) crumbled goat cheese

2 tablespoons (28 ml) extra virgin olive oil

1 lemon, halved

2 whole wheat pita bread (6 ½ -inch
   [16.5 cm]), warmed and halved

Serve this as an open-faced sandwich or overstuff a pita half. The choice is yours, just be sure you serve with tons of napkins if you decide to "overstuff!"

1. Combine the lentils, garlic, bay leaf, and water in the pressure cooker pot. Lock the lid in place and close the seal valve. Press the Manual button for 7 minutes.

2. Meanwhile, combine the kale mix, cucumber, onion, pepperoncini, crumbled goat cheese, extra virgin olive oil, and the juice of half a lemon in a medium bowl.

3. When the cook time ends, use a quick pressure release.

4. When the valve drops, carefully remove the lid. Drain the lentils in a fine-mesh sieve and run under cold water to cool quickly. Drain well, discarding the bay leaf, and stir the lentils into the kale mixture.

5. Spoon the lentil mixture into each pita half. Cut the remaining lemon half into wedges to serve alongside.

▸ **SERVES 4; 1¼ cups (163 g) lentil mixture plus ½ pita bread per serving**

▸ **NUTRITION FACTS**

Amount Per Serving		
Calories	330	
Calories from Fat	120	
		% Daily Value
Total Fat	13 g	20%
Saturated Fat	4.5 g	23%
Trans Fat	0 g	
Cholesterol	25 mg	8%
Sodium	470 mg	20%
Total Carbohydrate	40 g	13%
Dietary Fiber	8 g	32%
Sugars	3 g	
Protein	15 g	
Vitamin A		150%
Vitamin C		80%
Calcium		10%
Iron		40%
Magnesium	35 mg	
Potassium	309.67 mg	

Marinated Garbanzo Long Lettuce Wraps

6 ounces (170 g) dried chickpeas, rinsed

3 cups (700 ml) water

½ teaspoon dried rosemary leaves

¼ cup (40 g) chopped red onion

2 tablespoons (28 ml) apple cider vinegar

1½ tablespoons (25 ml) extra virgin olive oil

1 clove garlic, minced

2 teaspoons Dijon mustard

1½ teaspoons dried oregano

¼ teaspoon black pepper

½ teaspoon salt

2 avocados, peeled, pitted, and chopped

8 large romaine leaves

1 lemon, quartered

▸ **NUTRITION FACTS**

Amount Per Serving

		% Daily Value
Calories	330	
Calories from Fat	160	
Total Fat	18 g	28%
Saturated Fat	2 g	10%
Trans Fat	0 g	
Cholesterol	0 mg	0%
Sodium	370 mg	15%
Total Carbohydrate	36 g	12%
Dietary Fiber	14 g	56%
Sugars	6 g	
Protein		11 g
Vitamin A		70%
Vitamin C		45%
Calcium		6%
Iron		20%
Magnesium	21.37 mg	
Potassium	743.83 mg	

Tossing the beans while they're still hot allows the flavors of the other ingredients to penetrate deeper into the beans. This is a great make-ahead dish, too.

1. Combine the chickpeas, water, and rosemary in the pressure cooker pot. Lock the lid in place and close the seal valve. Press the Manual button for 35 minutes.

2. Meanwhile, combine the onion, apple cider vinegar, extra virgin olive oil, garlic, mustard, oregano, and pepper in a shallow pan, such as a glass pie pan.

3. When the cook time ends, use a 10-minute natural pressure release, then a quick pressure release.

4. When the valve drops, carefully remove the lid. Drain the chickpeas in a colander. Place the hot chickpeas in the onion mixture and stir until well coated. Cover and refrigerate for 1 hour or overnight.

5. Stir the salt into the chickpeas mixture, then gently stir in the avocado until just blended. Spoon the mixture evenly down the center of each leaf. Eat as you would a hot dog or a taco. Serve with lemon wedges.

▸ **SERVES 4; About ¾ cup (180 g) bean mixture plus 2 lettuce leaves per serving**

Knife-and-Fork Chipotle Pineapple Chicken Tortillas

1 pound (455 g) boneless, skinless chicken thighs

1 medium poblano chile pepper, sliced

1/2 cup (80 g) chopped onion

1 chipotle pepper in adobo sauce, minced

1/2 cup (85 g) pineapple tidbits, drained, reserving 1/4 cup (60 ml) juice

3/4 cup (175 ml) water

1 teaspoon smoked paprika

1/2 teaspoon ground cumin

1/2 teaspoon salt

1 tablespoon (13 g) sugar

8 corn tortillas

1/2 cup (8 g) chopped fresh cilantro

1/2 cup (115 g) reduce-fat sour cream

1 lime, quartered

No need to fold . . . no way, actually! These tortillas are piled high with heat, sweet, and freshness! If you DO decide to fold, be sure to serve with tons of napkins.

1. Combine the chicken, poblano pepper, onion, chipotle pepper, pineapple and reserved juice, water, paprika, cumin, and salt in the pressure cooker pot. Lock the lid in place and close the seal valve. Press the Cancel button and reset to Manual for 6 minutes.

2. When the cook time ends, use a 5-minute natural release, then a quick pressure release. When the valve drops, carefully remove the lid and check the chicken for doneness. Let it stand on a cutting board for 5 minutes, then shred. .

Amount Per Serving

Calories	340	
Calories from Fat	70	
		% Daily Value
Total Fat	8 g	12%
Saturated Fat	3 g	15%
Trans Fat	0 g	
Cholesterol	115 mg	38%
Sodium	470 mg	20%
Total Carbohydrate	40 g	13%
Dietary Fiber	4 g	16%
Sugars	14 g	
Protein	26 g	
Vitamin A		15%
Vitamin C		100%
Calcium		6%
Iron		8%
Magnesium	37.58 mg	
Potassium	441.20 mg	

3. Meanwhile, press the Cancel button. Select Browning/ Sauté. Bring to a boil and cook for 5 minutes, or until the juices are thickened slightly.

4. Add the shredded chicken and sugar to the pot, stir to combine, return to a boil, and cook for 2 to 3 minutes, or until the liquid has almost evaporated.

5. Serve on corn tortillas with cilantro and sour cream. Serve the lime wedges alongside.

► **SERVES 4; 1 cup (140 g) chicken mixture, 2 tortillas, and 2 tablespoon (30 g) sour cream per serving**

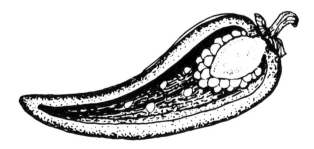

Shredded Pork Tortillas with Fresh Salsa

2 tablespoons (28 ml) canola oil

2 pounds (900 g) trimmed boneless pork shoulder, cut into 4 pieces

2 onions, thinly sliced (about 8 ounces [225 g] total)

1½ cups (355 ml) light beer, such as Miller Lite

2 tablespoons (28 ml) Worcestershire sauce

1 teaspoon garlic powder

1 tablespoon (6 g) ground cumin

1 teaspoon dried oregano leaves

½ teaspoon black pepper

½ teaspoon salt

16 corn tortillas

½ cup (130 g) fresh salsa

½ cup (115 g) nonfat plain Greek yogurt

2 avocados, peeled, pitted, and chopped

The pork in this dish is so tender, all you have to do is gently stir and it shreds . . . right in the pot!

1. Select Browning/Sauté on the pressure cooker. When the pot is hot, add the canola oil. Tilt the pot to coat the bottom lightly. Add half of the pork and cook for 3 minutes, turn, and cook for 3 minutes longer. Set aside on a separate plate. Repeat with the remaining pork.

2. Return the browned pork to the pressure cooker pot. Top with the onions, beer, Worcestershire sauce, garlic powder, cumin, oregano, and pepper and stir to combine. Lock the lid in place and close the seal valve. Press the Cancel button and reset to Manual for 75 minutes.

▸ NUTRITION FACTS

Amount Per Serving

Calories	390
Calories from Fat	170

		% Daily Value
Total Fat	19 g	29%
Saturated Fat	5 g	25%
Trans Fat	0 g	
Cholesterol	70 mg	23%
Sodium	320 mg	13%
Total Carbohydrate	32 g	11%
Dietary Fiber	6 g	24%
Sugars	5 g	
Protein	22 g	

Vitamin A		2%
Vitamin C		10%
Calcium		4%
Iron		10%
Magnesium	31.03 mg	
Potassium	482.93 mg	

3. When the cook time ends, use a quick pressure release.

4. When the valve drops, remove the lid carefully and check the pork for doneness. Strain the pork mixture in a colander, discarding the liquid. Return the strained pork mixture to the pot, sprinkle with the salt, and shred the pork in the pot.

5. Top the corn tortillas with the shredded pork mixture, salsa, yogurt and chopped avocado.

▸ **SERVES 8; About ½ cup pork (85 g), 1 tablespoon (16 g) salsa, 2 tortillas, ¼ (50 g) avocado, and 1 tablespoon (15 g) sour cream per serving**

Tender and Spiced Pork Sandwiches

1 tablespoon (15 ml) canola oil

2 pounds (900 g) trimmed boneless pork shoulder, cut into 4 pieces

2 cups (168 g) frozen peppers and onions

2/3 cup (160 ml) water

2 chipotle peppers in adobo sauce, minced

2 tablespoons (28 ml) Worcestershire sauce

1 teaspoon smoked paprika

1/2 teaspoon ground allspice

1 teaspoon ground cumin

1/2 cup (125 g) barbecue sauce

2 tablespoons (40 g) honey

8 whole wheat hamburger buns, warmed

▸ **NUTRITION FACTS**

Amount Per Serving

Calories	360	
Calories from Fat	130	

		% Daily Value
Total Fat	15 g	23%
Saturated Fat	5 g	25%
Trans Fat	0 g	
Cholesterol	70 mg	23%
Sodium	430 mg	18%
Total Carbohydrate	35 g	12%
Dietary Fiber	4 g	16%
Sugars	14 g	
Protein	22 g	

Vitamin A		6%
Vitamin C		0%
Calcium		6%
Iron		15%
Magnesium	53.07 mg	
Potassium	346.22 mg	

This pork literally falls apart as you remove it from the pot, and it's unbelievably tender. By spooning the sauce on top of the pork instead of mixing the sauce in, you get the full taste and aroma of the pork with layers of flavor. Try the pork mixture with other sauces as well.

1. Select Browning/Sauté on the pressure cooker. When the pot is hot, add the canola oil and tilt the pot to coat the bottom lightly. Add half of the pork and cook without stirring for 5 minutes. Remove to a plate. Repeat with the remaining pork.

2. Return the pork to the pressure cooker pot. Add the peppers and onions, water, chipotle peppers, Worcestershire sauce, paprika, allspice, and cumin and stir to combine. Lock the lid in place and close the seal valve. Press the Cancel button and reset to Manual for 75 minutes.

3. Meanwhile, combine the barbecue sauce with the honey in a small bowl.

4. When the cook time ends, use a quick pressure release.

5. When the valve drops, carefully remove the lid test the pork for doneness. Remove the pork mixture with a slotted spoon. Roughly shred the pork. Serve on the hamburger buns and spoon equal amounts of the sauce on top.

▸ **SERVES 8; 1/2 cup (85 g) pork mixture, about 1 tablespoon sauce (23 g), and 1 bun per serving**

Shred-in-the-Pot Beef Po'boys

1 tablespoon (15 ml) canola oil

2 pounds (900 g) trimmed flat half beef brisket, cut into 8 pieces

1½ cups (240 g) chopped onion

1 can (14.5 ounces [410 g]) no-salt-added diced tomatoes

¾ cup (175 ml) water

3 tablespoons (45 ml) balsamic vinegar

1 teaspoon garlic powder

1 teaspoon dried thyme

Black pepper to taste

¼ cup (60 ml) reduced-sodium soy sauce

1 tablespoon (13 g) sugar

12 ounces (340 g) multigrain Italian loaf bread, cut into 8 slices

This beef mixture can be shredded right in the pot. It's even better the next day and freezes well, too!

1. Pat the beef dry with paper towels. Select Browning/ Sauté on the pressure cooker. When the pot is hot, add the canola oil and tilt the pot to coat the bottom lightly. Add half of the beef in a single layer and cook for 3 minutes on each side. Remove the beef and set aside on a plate. Repeat with the remaining beef.

2. Return the beef and any accumulated juices to the pressure cooker pot. Stir in the onions, tomatoes, water, balsamic vinegar, garlic powder, and thyme. Lock the lid in place and close the seal valve. Press the Cancel button and reset to Manual for 55 minutes.

3. When the cook time ends, use a quick pressure release.

4. When the valve drops, carefully remove the lid. Check the beef for doneness. Strain the beef mixture in a colander (discard the liquid). Return the strained beef mixture to the pot. Turn off the heat. Add the soy sauce, sugar, and black pepper. Stir until the beef is shredded. Serve over the sliced Italian bread slices.

▸ **SERVES 8; ½ cup (103 g) beef mixture and 1½ ounces (43 g) bread per serving**

▸ **NUTRITION FACTS**

Amount Per Serving		
Calories	300	
Calories from Fat	80	
		% Daily Value
Total Fat	8 g	12%
Saturated Fat	2 g	10%
Trans Fat	0 g	
Cholesterol	70 mg	23%
Sodium	410 mg	17%
Total Carbohydrate	28 g	9%
Dietary Fiber	4 g	16%
Sugars	7 g	
Protein	29 g	
Vitamin A		6%
Vitamin C		20%
Calcium		8%
Iron		20%
Magnesium	21.33 mg	
Potassium	469.13 mg	

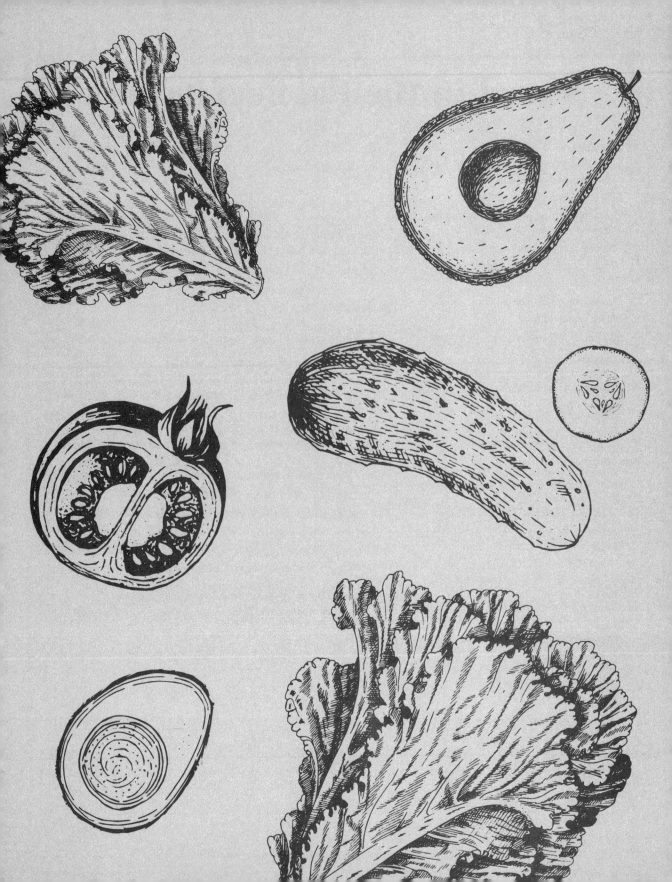

2

Substantial Salads

Citrusy Beet and Goat Cheese Salad

DRESSING:

2 tablespoons (28 ml) white balsamic vinegar

1 tablespoon (15 ml) canola oil

1 tablespoon (20 g) honey

1/2 teaspoon orange zest

1/4 teaspoon crushed red pepper flakes

1/8 teaspoon salt

SALAD:

3 large beets with greens (about 1 1/4 pounds [570 g] total)

2 ounces (56 g) slivered almonds

1 cup (235 ml) water

3 cups (90 g) baby spinach

2 ounces (55 g) thinly sliced red onion

1 navel orange, peeled and cut into sections

4 ounces (115 g) crumbled goat cheese

Fresh beets are loaded with rich nutrients, but we don't eat enough because the juices stain everything, including our fingers. The time it takes to cook them is a problem, too. But with the techniques used in this recipe, you'll want to serve them on the busiest days—it's that easy. They add "meatiness" and rich body to any dish, too!

1. To make the dressing: Whisk together the dressing ingredients in a small bowl and set aside.

2. To make the salad: Rinse the beets and beet greens. Cut off the stems, reserving the beet greens (discard the stems). Pat the beet greens dry and tear into bite-size pieces.

3. Select Browning/Sauté on the pressure cooker. When the pot is hot, add the almonds and cook for 4 minutes, stirring occasionally; remove from the pot and set aside on a plate.

Cook's Note:

When working with beets, rinse your hands often to prevent staining.

Amount Per Serving

Calories	300	
Calories from Fat	160	

		% Daily Value
Total Fat	18 g	28%
Saturated Fat	5 g	25%
Trans Fat	0 g	
Cholesterol	35 mg	12%
Sodium	360 mg	15%
Total Carbohydrate	27 g	9%
Dietary Fiber	8 g	32%
Sugars	17 g	
Protein	11 g	

Vitamin A		50%
Vitamin C		60%
Calcium		15%
Iron		15%
Magnesium	100.76 mg	
Potassium	684.59 mg	

4. Add the water and steamer basket to the pressure cooker pot. Place the beets in the basket. Lock the lid in place and close the seal valve. Press the Cancel button, then reset to Manual for 20 minutes.

5. When the cook time ends, use a quick pressure release.

6. When the valve drops, carefully remove the lid. Place the beets in a colander and run under cold water until cool enough to handle. Hold a beet under water while slipping the peel off with your fingertips. Repeat with the remaining beets. Cut each beet into 8 wedges. Let cool completely. (Note: If time is short, place the wedges in a colander and run under cold water for 1 minute to cool quickly.)

7. Arrange the spinach and beet greens on each of 4 dinner plates. Top with the beets, onions, and orange sections. Drizzle the dressing evenly over all and top with the goat cheese and toasted almonds.

▸ **SERVES 4; About 2½ cups (235 g) salad per serving**

Baby Spinach and Asparagus Salad with Eggs

SALAD:

2 cups (475 ml) water

6 large eggs

12 ounces (340 g) asparagus, ends trimmed and cut into 2-inch (5 cm) pieces

6 cups (180 g) baby spinach

½ cup (80 g) chopped red onion

DRESSING:

¼ cup (60 ml) white balsamic vinegar

2 tablespoons (28 ml) canola oil

1 tablespoon (20 g) honey

1 teaspoon Dijon mustard

½ teaspoon salt

You'll never want to cook hard-boiled eggs any other way once you've experienced this "easy-to-peel" method— the shells just slip right off.

1. To make the salad: Add the water and a steamer basket to the pressure cooker pot and place the eggs in the steamer basket. Lock the lid in place and close the seal valve. Press the Manual button for 7 minutes. Meanwhile, prepare an ice bath in a medium bowl and set aside.

2. When the cook time ends, use a quick pressure release.

3. When the valve drops, carefully remove the lid. Remove the eggs with tongs or a large spoon. Immediately place in the ice water and let stand for 3 minutes before peeling and chopping the eggs.

4. Place the asparagus in the steamer basket. Lock the lid in place and close the seal valve. Press the Cancel button and reset to Manual for 1 minute.

▸ NUTRITION FACTS

Amount Per Serving

Calories	240	
Calories from Fat	130	
		% Daily Value
Total Fat	14 g	22%
Saturated Fat	3 g	15%
Trans Fat	0 g	
Cholesterol	280 mg	93%
Sodium	460 mg	19%
Total Carbohydrate	15 g	5%
Dietary Fiber	3 g	12%
Sugars	9 g	
Protein	12 g	
Vitamin A		60%
Vitamin C		35%
Calcium		10%
Iron		15%
Magnesium	38.75 mg	
Potassium	366.14 mg	

5. When the cook time ends, use a quick pressure release.

6. When the valve drops, carefully remove the lid. Remove the asparagus and steamer basket and run under cold water to quickly cool. Drain well.

7. Arrange the spinach on each of 4 plates. Top with the asparagus, chopped eggs, and onion.

8. To make the dressing: Whisk together the dressing ingredients in a small bowl and drizzle evenly over the salads.

▸ **SERVES 4; About 2½ cups (213 g) salad per serving**

Wheat Berry, Black Bean, and Dried Cherry Salad

2 ounces (55 g) chopped pecans

2 ounces (55 g) dried black beans

½ cup (90 g) wheat berries

4 cups (946 ml) water

1 cup (120 g) sliced celery

½ cup (80 g) chopped red onion

½ cup (80 g) dried cherries

2 tablespoons (28 ml) white
   balsamic vinegar

1 tablespoon (15 ml) extra virgin olive oil

¼ teaspoon crushed red pepper flakes

¼ teaspoon salt

2 ounces (55 g) crumbled reduced-fat
   blue cheese

4 cups (80 g) arugula, optional

Colorful and jam-packed with flavor and texture, this salad is great all year long!

1. Select Browning/Sauté on the pressure cooker. When the pot is hot, add the pecans and cook for 5 minutes, stirring occasionally. Transfer to a medium bowl and set aside.

2. Place the black beans and wheat berries in a fine-mesh sieve, rinse, and drain. Place in the pressure cooker pot along with the water. Lock the lid in place and close the seal valve. Press the Cancel button and reset to Manual for 25 minutes.

3. Meanwhile, combine the toasted pecans, celery, onion, dried cherries, white balsamic vinegar, extra virgin olive oil, red pepper flakes, and salt in a medium bowl.

Cook's Note:
This is a great make-ahead dish, as it holds well. For a slightly sweeter salad, add 2 teaspoons sugar when making the dressing.

▸ NUTRITION FACTS

Amount Per Serving

Calories	390	
Calories from Fat	150	
		% Daily Value
Total Fat	17 g	26%
Saturated Fat	3 g	15%
Trans Fat	0 g	
Cholesterol	10 mg	3%
Sodium	360 mg	15%
Total Carbohydrate	48 g	16%
Dietary Fiber	9 g	36%
Sugars	19 g	
Protein	12 g	
Vitamin A		15%
Vitamin C		10%
Calcium		15%
Iron		15%
Magnesium	26.33 mg	
Potassium	440.82 mg	

4. When the cook time ends, use a quick pressure release.

5. When the valve drops, carefully remove the lid. Drain the black beans and wheat berries in a fine-mesh sieve and run under cold water. Add to the bowl and toss to combine. Add the blue cheese and toss gently. Serve over arugula, if desired.

▸ **SERVES 4; 1 cup (170 g) bean mixture per serving**

Turmeric Buckwheat and Garbanzo Salad

2 ounces (55 g) chopped pecans

1 3/4 cups (410 ml) water

3/4 cup (138 g) buckwheat groats, rinsed

3/4 teaspoon ground turmeric

1 1/2 cups (183 g) matchstick carrots

1/2 cup (80 g) chopped red onion

2 cups (40 g) arugula

1/2 can (15 ounces [420 g]) no-salt-added chickpeas, rinsed

1/2 cup (89 g) pitted and chopped dates (about 4)

3/4 cup (12 g) chopped fresh cilantro

2 tablespoons (28 ml) canola oil

3 tablespoons (45 ml) white balsamic vinegar

1 1/2 teaspoons ground cumin

1/2 teaspoon salt

1/4 teaspoon crushed red pepper flakes, optional

With the name "buckwheat groats," you would think this is a grain and contains wheat . . . but it's neither. Buckwheat groats are the hearty hulled seeds from the leafy buckwheat plant. They're actually a fruit and are gluten free. Buckwheat groats are sold in major grocery stores and health food stores in packages and in bulk form.

1. Select Browning/Sauté on the pressure cooker. When the pot is hot, add the pecans and cook for 4 minutes, stirring occasionally. Transfer to a medium bowl and set aside.

2. Add the water, buckwheat groats, and turmeric to the pressure cooker pot. Lock the lid in place and close the seal valve. Press the Cancel button and reset to Manual for 2 minutes.

3. Meanwhile, add the carrots, onion, arugula, chickpeas, dates, cilantro, canola oil, white balsamic vinegar, cumin, salt, and crushed red pepper flakes to the bowl with the toasted pecans and toss to combine.

Amount Per Serving

Calories	360
Calories from Fat	160

		% Daily Value
Total Fat	18 g	28%
Saturated Fat	1.5 g	8%
Trans Fat	0 g	
Cholesterol	0 mg	0%
Sodium	340 mg	14%
Total Carbohydrate	46 g	15%
Dietary Fiber	9 g	36%
Sugars	9 g	
Protein	9 g	

Vitamin A		160%
Vitamin C		10%
Calcium		8%
Iron		10%
Magnesium	109.99 mg	
Potassium	521.92 mg	

4. When the cook time ends, use a natural pressure release for 5 minutes, then a quick pressure release.

5. When the valve drops, carefully remove the lid. Place the buckwheat mixture in a fine-mesh sieve and run under cold water to cool quickly. Drain well. Add to the pecan mixture and toss until well blended. Serve immediately for best flavor and texture.

▸ **SERVES 4; 1½ cups (about 210 g) per serving**

Farro-Pepperoncini Salad

2 cups (475 ml) water

3/4 cup (156 g) uncooked pearled farro

2 tablespoons (28 ml) extra virgin olive oil, divided

2 cups (134 g) shredded kale

1 cup (180 g) grape tomatoes, quartered

1/2 cup (80 g) finely chopped red onion

1/4 cup (10 g) chopped fresh basil

2 ounces (55 g) pepperoncini, sliced

2 tablespoons (28 ml) red wine vinegar

1/4 teaspoon salt

1 avocado, peeled, pitted, and chopped

1/4 cup (38 g) crumbled reduced-fat feta cheese

Bite into this intriguingly fresh and bountiful salad and find out why farro will become your go-to ancient grain.

1. Combine the water, farro, and 2 teaspoons extra virgin olive oil in the pressure cooker pot. Lock the lid in place and close the seal valve. Press the Manual button for 8 minutes.

2. Meanwhile, combine the kale, tomatoes, onion, basil, pepperoncini, red wine vinegar, salt, and remaining 4 teaspoons extra virgin olive oil in a medium bowl.

3. When the cook time ends, use a quick pressure release.

4. When the valve drops, carefully remove the lid. Drain the farro in a fine-mesh sieve and run under cold running water to cool quickly; drain well. Add the drained farro and avocado to the kale mixture and gently stir until blended. Sprinkle evenly with the crumbled feta cheese.

▶ **SERVES 4; 1³/4 cups (184 g) per serving**

▶ **NUTRITION FACTS**

Amount Per Serving

		% Daily Value
Calories	330	
Calories from Fat	150	
Total Fat	17 g	26%
Saturated Fat	3 g	15%
Trans Fat	0 g	
Cholesterol	5 mg	2%
Sodium	470 mg	20%
Total Carbohydrate	38 g	13%
Dietary Fiber	9 g	36%
Sugars	3 g	
Protein	10 g	
Vitamin A		80%
Vitamin C		90%
Calcium		10%
Iron		15%
Magnesium	36.42 mg	
Potassium	536.76 mg	

Cook's Note:
Serve immediately or cover and refrigerate overnight. You may want to add 1 to 2 teaspoons more vinegar if not serving immediately.

Fresh Ginger Lentil Salad with Cilantro

2 ounces (55 g) slivered almonds

3/4 cup (144 g) dried brown lentils, rinsed

2 cups (475 ml) water

3/4 cup (120 g) finely chopped red onion

1/2 cup (8 g) chopped fresh cilantro

1 tablespoon (13 g) sugar

2 tablespoons (28 ml) reduced-sodium soy sauce

2 tablespoons (28 ml) apple cider vinegar

2 teaspoons grated fresh ginger

1/4 teaspoon crushed red pepper flakes

1/4 teaspoon salt

1 cup (150 g) shelled edamame

▸ **NUTRITION FACTS**

Amount Per Serving

Calories	290	
Calories from Fat	80	
		% Daily Value
Total Fat	9 g	14%
Saturated Fat	0.5 g	3%
Trans Fat	0 g	
Cholesterol	0 mg	0%
Sodium	450 mg	19%
Total Carbohydrate	37 g	12%
Dietary Fiber	8 g	32%
Sugars	6 g	
Protein	17 g	
Vitamin A		8%
Vitamin C		10%
Calcium		8%
Iron		20%
Magnesium	59.52 mg	
Potassium	411.52 mg	

Use lentils in your salads instead of rice or pasta for a nutritional boost and a new flavor and texture twist.

1. Select Browning/Sauté on the pressure cooker. When the pot is hot, add the almonds and cook for 4 minutes, stirring occasionally. Transfer to a medium bowl and set aside.

2. Combine the lentils and water in the pressure cooker pot. Lock the lid in place and close the seal valve. Press the Cancel button and reset to Manual for 6 minutes.

3. Meanwhile, add the onion, cilantro, sugar, soy sauce, apple cider vinegar, ginger, red pepper flakes, and salt to the bowl with the toasted almonds and toss to combine.

4. When the cook time ends, use a quick pressure release.

5. When the valve drops, carefully remove the lid. Add the edamame to the lentils in the pot and let stand for 1 minute. Transfer the lentil mixture to a colander and run under cold running water to cool quickly. Drain well.

6. Add the lentil mixture to the almond mixture and stir until just blended. Serve immediately or cover and refrigerate overnight.

▸ **SERVES 4; 1 cup (184 g) per serving**

Spiced Salmon on Greens with Sesame Seed Dressing

FISH:

2 tablespoons (16 g) sesame seeds

1 cup (235 ml) water

2 salmon fillets (6 ounces [70 g] each) fresh or frozen

¼ teaspoon paprika

¼ teaspoon allspice

6 cups (180 to 402 g) torn mixed greens, such as kale, chard, and spinach

¼ cup (25 g) chopped green onion

¼ cup (40 g) dried cherries or (30 g) cranberries

DRESSING:

2 tablespoons (28 ml) balsamic vinegar

2 tablespoons (28 ml) canola oil

2 tablespoons (40 g) honey

1½ tablespoons (25 ml) reduced-sodium soy sauce

1 tablespoon (15 ml) Worcestershire sauce

¼ teaspoon crushed red pepper flakes

If you're trying to incorporate more salmon into your diet, but not really a big fan of salmon, then this dish is for you. The dressing includes soy sauce, honey, a bit of Worcestershire sauce, and a kick of heat, the perfect foil for the tender fish.

1. Select Browning/Sauté on the pressure cooker. When the pot is hot, add the sesame seeds and cook for 4 minutes, or until beginning to lightly brown, stirring occasionally. Transfer to a small bowl and set aside.

2. To make the fish: Add the water and a steamer basket to the pressure cooker pot, place the salmon in the basket, and sprinkle evenly with the paprika and allspice. Lock the lid in place and close the seal valve. Press the Cancel button and reset to Manual for 3 minutes.

Amount Per Serving

Calories	300	
Calories from Fat	140	
		% Daily Value
Total Fat	15 g	23%
Saturated Fat	2 g	10%
Trans Fat	0 g	
Cholesterol	45 mg	15%
Sodium	330 mg	14%
Total Carbohydrate	20 g	7%
Dietary Fiber	2 g	8%
Sugars	15 g	
Protein	20 g	
Vitamin A		45%
Vitamin C		25%
Calcium		20%
Iron		10%
Magnesium	44.50 mg	
Potassium	724.14 mg	

3. When the cook time ends, use a quick pressure release.

4. When the valve drops, carefully remove the lid. Check the salmon for doneness. Remove the salmon and place on a plate to cool, about 10 minutes.

5. Arrange equal amounts of the mixed greens on each of 4 dinner plates. Flake the salmon and place equal amounts on each serving of lettuce. Top with the green onion and dried fruit.

6. To make the dressing: Whisk together the dressing ingredients in a small bowl until well blended. Spoon evenly over the fish and mixed greens. Sprinkle evenly with the toasted sesame seeds.

▸ **SERVES 4; 2.3 ounces (65 g) salmon, 1½ cups (51 g) salad, and 2 tablespoons (28 ml) dressing per serving**

Dilled Shrimp and Pasta Salad

2 ounces (55 g) uncooked whole-grain rotini pasta

4 cups (940 ml) water

½ cup (50 g) sliced celery

⅓ cup (55 g) chopped red onion

¼ cup (60 g) light mayonnaise

2 teaspoons grated lemon zest

2 tablespoons (28 ml) lemon juice

2 teaspoons dried dill

½ teaspoon seafood seasoning, such as Old Bay

¼ teaspoon salt

1 pound (454 g) raw peeled shrimp

2 medium tomatoes, cut into 4 slices each (8 ounces [225 g] total)

This dish is fresh, fast, and exploding with flavor. Using lemon zest ups the lemony flavor without the tartness you would get from using too much lemon juice.

1. Combine the pasta and water in the pressure cooker pot. Lock the lid in place and close the seal valve. Press the Manual button for 3 minutes.

2. Meanwhile, combine the celery, onion, mayonnaise, lemon zest, lemon juice, dill, seafood seasoning, and salt in a medium bowl.

3. When the cook time ends, use a quick pressure release.

4. When the valve drops, carefully remove the lid. Stir in the shrimp. Lock the lid in place and close the seal valve. Press the Cancel button and reset to Manual for 1 minute.

5. When cook time ends, use a quick pressure release.

6. When the valve drops, carefully remove the lid. Check the shrimp for doneness. Drain the pasta and shrimp in a colander and run under cold water to cool quickly. Drain well and stir into the celery mixture. Serve over the sliced tomatoes.

▸ **SERVES 4; 1 cup (142 g) plus 2 ounces (55 g) tomatoes per serving**

▸ **NUTRITION FACTS**

Amount Per Serving

Calories	210	
Calories from Fat	60	
		% Daily Value
Total Fat	6 g	9%
Saturated Fat	1 g	5%
Trans Fat	0 g	
Cholesterol	190 mg	63%
Sodium	490 mg	20%
Total Carbohydrate	15 g	5%
Dietary Fiber	2 g	8%
Sugars	3 g	
Protein	26 g	
Vitamin A		10%
Vitamin C		20%
Calcium		10%
Iron		8%
Magnesium	49.26 mg	
Potassium	495.52 mg	

Tuna and Egg Salad on Sliced Cucumber

1 cup (235 ml) water

6 large eggs

3/4 cup (75 g) chopped celery

1/4 cup (40 g) chopped red onion

1 jalapeño, minced

1/4 cup (60 g) light mayonnaise

1 tablespoon (11 g) yellow mustard

1 tablespoon (15 ml) apple cider vinegar

2 teaspoons sugar

1/4 teaspoon salt

1 medium cucumber, thinly sliced

2 pouches (2.6 ounces [73 g] each)
   reduced-sodium chunk light tuna in water

In this recipe, you're only using four whole eggs plus the whites of the other two eggs. That helps add bulk and texture to the salad while keeping the cholesterol down.

1. Place a trivet in the pressure cooker pot and add the water. Place the eggs on the trivet. Lock the lid in place and close the seal valve. Press the Manual button for 7 minutes. Meanwhile, prepare an ice bath in a medium bowl and set aside.

2. When the cook time ends, use a quick pressure release.

3. When the valve drops, carefully remove the lid. Remove the eggs with tongs or a large spoon. Immediately place in the ice water and let stand for 3 minutes.

4. Meanwhile, combine the celery, onion, jalapeño, mayonnaise, mustard, apple cider vinegar, sugar, and salt in a medium bowl. Stir until well blended.

5. Peel the eggs and discard 2 of the egg yolks. Chop the remaining eggs and egg whites and add to the mayonnaise mixture. Gently stir until well blended. Spoon onto the cucumber slices. Flake the tuna and sprinkle evenly over all.

▸ **SERVES 4; 2/3 cup (111 g) egg salad, 1.3 ounces (36 g) tuna, and 2 ounces (55 g) cucumber per serving**

▸ **NUTRITION FACTS**

Amount Per Serving		% Daily Value
Calories	210	
Calories from Fat	100	
Total Fat	11 g	17%
Saturated Fat	3 g	15%
Trans Fat	0 g	
Cholesterol	205 mg	68%
Sodium	490 mg	18%
Total Carbohydrate	8 g	3%
Dietary Fiber	1 g	4%
Sugars	5 g	
Protein	18 g	
Vitamin A		10%
Vitamin C		15%
Calcium		6%
Iron		10%
Magnesium	25.39 mg	
Potassium	261.53 mg	

Curried Chicken-Almond Salad on Kiwi

2 ounces (55 g) slivered almonds

12 ounces (340 g) boneless, skinless chicken thighs

2 cups (475 ml) water

1 cup (100 g) chopped celery

½ cup (75 g) finely chopped red bell pepper

2 tablespoons (20 g) finely chopped red onion

½ cup (75 g) raisins, preferably golden

½ cup (115 g) light mayonnaise

2 tablespoons (28 ml) lime juice

2 teaspoons curry powder

2 teaspoons honey

¼ teaspoon ground cumin

¼ teaspoon salt

4 kiwi, peeled and sliced

▸ **NUTRITION FACTS**

Amount Per Serving

Calories	380	
Calories from Fat	160	
		% Daily Value
Total Fat	18 g	28%
Saturated Fat	2.5 g	13%
Trans Fat	0 g	
Cholesterol	85 mg	28%
Sodium	500 mg	21%
Total Carbohydrate	36 g	12%
Dietary Fiber	5 g	20%
Sugars	23 g	
Protein	22 g	
Vitamin A		15%
Vitamin C		150%
Calcium		10%
Iron		10%
Magnesium	82.71 mg	
Potassium	792.55 mg	

The crunch from the celery, sweetness from the fruit, and nuttiness from the toasted almonds all come together while the color of the dish slowly turns from creamy white to soft yellow, all on its own.

1. Select Browning/Sauté on the pressure cooker. When the pot is hot, add the almonds and cook for 4 minutes, stirring occasionally. Transfer to a plate and set aside.

2. Combine the chicken and water in the pressure cooker pot. Lock the lid in place and close the seal valve. Press the Cancel button and reset to Manual for 6 minutes.

3. When the cook time ends, use a natural pressure release for 5 minutes, then a quick pressure release.

4. When the valve drops, carefully remove the lid. Check the chicken for doneness. Place the chicken on a cutting board and let stand for 5 minutes before chopping. Discard the liquid in the pot.

5. Meanwhile, combine the celery, bell pepper, onion, raisins, mayonnaise, lime juice, curry powder, cumin, and salt in a medium bowl. Add the chicken and stir until well blended. Cover and refrigerate for 1 hour to allow the flavors to blend and the curry to turn a soft yellow color.

6. Serve the salad on the kiwi slices with the toasted almonds sprinkled over top.

▸ **SERVES 4; 1 cup (171 g) salad plus 1 kiwi (76 g) per serving**

Chicken, Cherry, and Toasted Pecan Kale Salad

2 ounces (55 g) chopped pecans

2 cups (475 ml) water

2 boneless, skinless chicken breasts (8-ounce [225 g] each)

1 teaspoon curry powder

1/4 teaspoon black pepper

3 tablespoons (45 ml) reduced-sodium soy sauce

1 tablespoon (20 g) honey or (13 g) sugar

1 to 2 teaspoons orange zest

4 cups (170 g) kale and spinach mix

1 1/3 cups (207 g) pitted dark sweet cherries (fresh or frozen, thawed), coarsely chopped

1 cup (122 g) matchstick carrots

1/3 cup (33 g) finely chopped green onion

The combination of the ingredients in this salad explodes with flavor . . . and potassium.

1. Select Browning/Sauté on the pressure cooker. When the pot is hot, add the pecans and cook for 5 minutes, stirring occasionally. Transfer to a plate and set aside.

2. Place a trivet in the pressure cooker pot and add the water. Top with the chicken and sprinkle with the curry powder and pepper.

3. Lock the lid in place and close the seal valve. Press the Cancel button and reset to Manual for 6 minutes.

4. When the cook time ends, use a 5-minute natural pressure release.

5. When the valve drops, carefully remove the lid. Check the chicken for doneness. Place the chicken on a cutting board and let stand for 5 minutes before chopping. Discard the liquid in the pot.

6. In a small bowl, combine the soy sauce, honey, and orange zest and whisk until well blended.

7. Place equal amounts of the kale and spinach mix in each of 4 bowls. Top with the chicken, cherries, carrots, green onion, and toasted pecans. Spoon the soy sauce mixture over all.

▸ **SERVES 4; 1 cup (43 g) kale mix, 3 ounces (85 g) chicken, and 3/4 cup (77 g) toppings per serving**

▸ **NUTRITION FACTS**

Amount Per Serving

Calories	320	
Calories from Fat	120	
		% Daily Value
Total Fat	13 g	20%
Saturated Fat	1.5 g	8%
Trans Fat	0 g	
Cholesterol	85 mg	28%
Sodium	420 mg	18%
Total Carbohydrate	21 g	7%
Dietary Fiber	5 g	20%
Sugars	14 g	
Protein	30 g	
Vitamin A		130%
Vitamin C		25%
Calcium		15%
Iron		8%
Magnesium	62.56 mg	
Potassium	1166.77 mg	

Cilantro Chicken–Avocado Salad on Tomato Slices

¼ cup (35 g) hulled, roasted, salted pumpkin seeds

2 cups (475 ml) water

12 ounces (340 g) boneless, skinless chicken breast

½ teaspoon ground cumin

1 cup (135 g) chopped cucumber

½ cup (80 g) chopped red onion

2 tablespoons (28 ml) lime juice

1 tablespoon (15 ml) extra virgin olive oil

1 clove garlic, minced

½ teaspoon salt

1 avocado, peeled, pitted, and chopped

½ cup (8 g) chopped cilantro

2 medium tomatoes, cut into 12 slices total

1 lime, cut into 4 wedges, optional

Tomatoes are not always in peak season, so when that happens, use a pint of sweet grape tomatoes instead. Just cut them in half and serve alongside the salad for a fresh, bright addition.

1. Select Browning/Sauté on the pressure cooker. When the pot is hot, add the pumpkin seeds and cook for 4 minutes, stirring occasionally. Transfer to a plate and set aside.

2. Pour the water into the pressure cooker pot. Add the chicken and sprinkle with the cumin. Lock the lid in place and close the seal valve. Press the Cancel button, then reset to Manual for 6 minutes.

3. When the cook time ends, use a 5-minute natural pressure release.

Amount Per Serving

Calories	260	
Calories from Fat	130	
		% Daily Value
Total Fat	15 g	23%
Saturated Fat	2.5 g	13%
Trans Fat	0 g	
Cholesterol	60 mg	20%
Sodium	360 mg	15%
Total Carbohydrate	10 g	3%
Dietary Fiber	4 g	16%
Sugars	3 g	
Protein	23 g	
Vitamin A		15%
Vitamin C		35%
Calcium		4%
Iron		10%
Magnesium	0.46 mg	
Potassium	301.32 mg	

4. When the valve drops, carefully remove the lid. Check the chicken for doneness. Place the chicken on a cutting board and let stand for 5 minutes before chopping. Discard the liquid in the pot.

5. Meanwhile, combine the cucumber, onion, lime juice, extra virgin olive oil, garlic, and salt in a medium bowl; stir until well blended. Gently stir in the chopped chicken, avocado, and cilantro and serve over the tomato slices, sprinkled with the toasted pumpkin seeds, and with the lime wedges, if desired.

▶ **SERVES 4; ³/4 cup (120.5 g) chicken mixture plus 3 tomato slices (45 g) per serving**

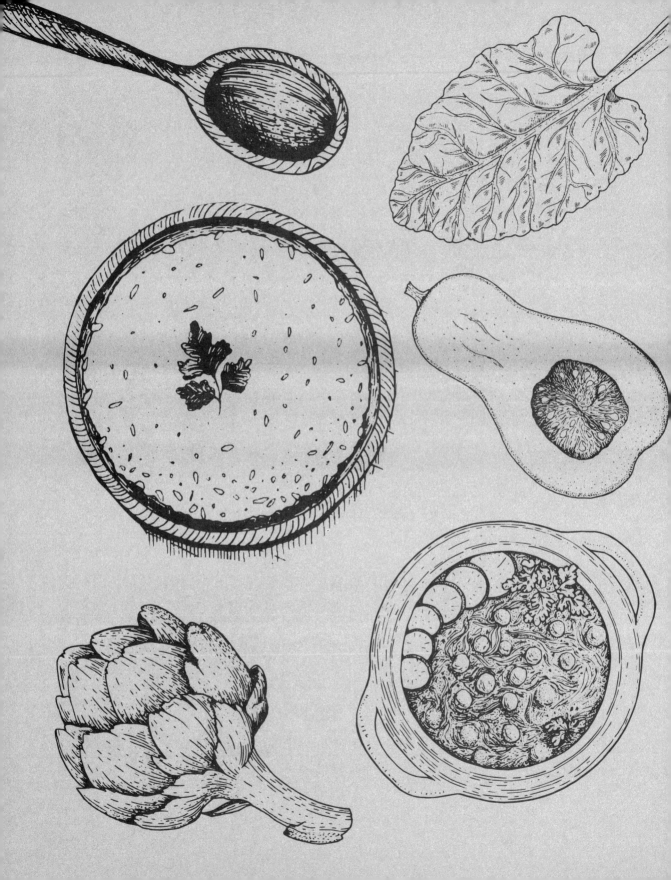

3

Soups, Chilis, Stews, and Bowls

Cheesy Veggie Chowder

1 tablespoon (15 ml) canola oil

1 cup (160 g) chopped onion

1 pound (455 g) red potatoes, cut into ½-inch (1.3 cm) cubes

1½ cups (177 g) chopped poblano peppers

1½ cups (246 g) frozen corn

1 cup (235 ml) water

¼ teaspoon black pepper

⅛ teaspoon cayenne pepper

2 ounces (55 g) reduced-fat cream cheese, cut into small cubes

¾ cup (175 ml) 2% milk

1 teaspoon seafood seasoning, such as Old Bay

¼ teaspoon salt

3 ounces (85 g) shredded reduced-fat sharp cheddar cheese, divided

¼ cup (25 g) finely chopped green onion

No need to peel the potatoes, no need to thaw the corn—just toss them in the pressure cooker and get creamy chowder in minutes.

1. Select Browning/Sauté on the pressure cooker. When the pot is hot, add the canola oil to the pot. Tilt the pot to coat the bottom lightly. Add the onion and cook for 4 minutes, or until beginning to lightly brown.

2. Stir in the potatoes, poblano peppers, corn, water, black pepper, and cayenne pepper. Lock the lid in place and close the seal valve. Press the Cancel button and reset to Manual for 3 minutes.

3. When the cook time ends, use a quick pressure release.

4. When the valve drops, carefully remove the lid. Stir in the cream cheese, milk, seafood seasoning, salt, and half of the cheddar cheese. Serve topped with equal amounts of the remaining cheddar cheese and the green onions.

▸ **SERVES 4; About 1¼ cups (323 g) per serving**

▸ **NUTRITION FACTS**

Amount Per Serving

Calories	320	
Calories from Fat	110	
		% Daily Value
Total Fat	13 g	20%
Saturated Fat	5 g	25%
Trans Fat	0 g	
Cholesterol	30 mg	10%
Sodium	540 mg	23%
Total Carbohydrate	42 g	14%
Dietary Fiber	5 g	20%
Sugars	10 g	
Protein	14 g	
Vitamin A		20%
Vitamin C		260%
Calcium		25%
Iron		10%
Magnesium	64.38 mg	
Potassium	990.76 mg	

Curried Garbanzo Bowls

2 tablespoons (28 ml) canola oil

1 cup (160 g) chopped onion

1 can (8 ounces [225 g]) no-salt-added tomato sauce

1 tablespoon (6 g) curry powder

1 teaspoon garam masala

2 bay leaves

1/4 teaspoon cayenne pepper

3 cups (700 ml) water

6 ounces (170 g) dried chickpeas, rinsed

1 package (12 ounces [340 g]) frozen riced sweet potatoes and cauliflower

1 1/2 to 2 tablespoons (20 to 26 g) sugar

2 tablespoons (28 ml) lemon juice

3/4 teaspoon salt

Chopped fresh cilantro

▶ NUTRITION FACTS

Amount Per Serving

Calories	310	
Calories from Fat	90	
		% Daily Value
Total Fat	10 g	15%
Saturated Fat	0.5 g	3%
Trans Fat	0 g	
Cholesterol	0 mg	0%
Sodium	490 mg	20%
Total Carbohydrate	48 g	16%
Dietary Fiber	11 g	44%
Sugars	16 g	
Protein	11 g	
Vitamin A		130%
Vitamin C		60%
Calcium		8%
Iron		20%
Magnesium	29.98 mg	
Potassium	873.83 mg	

Adding frozen riced vegetables to this dish at the end gives a thick, chili-like texture. If the frozen riced veggies are solid and can't easily be separated, just place the bag on the kitchen counter and hit it with a can or heavy spoon to loosen the veggies before adding them to the pot.

1. Press Browning/Sauté on the pressure cooker. When the pot is hot, add the canola oil and tilt the pot to coat the bottom lightly. Add the onion and cook for 5 minutes, stirring frequently.

2. Add the tomato sauce, curry powder, garam masala, bay leaves, and cayenne pepper. Cook for 3 minutes, or until the sauce begins to separate slightly. Add the water and chickpeas. Lock the lid in place and close the seal valve. Press the Cancel button and reset to Manual for 45 minutes.

3. When the cook time ends, use a 10-minute natural pressure release, then a quick pressure release.

4. When the valve drops, carefully remove the lid. Stir in the riced vegetable. Lock the lid in place and close the seal valve. Press the Cancel button and reset to Manual for 3 minutes.

5. When the cook time ends, use a quick pressure release.

6. When the valve drops, carefully remove the lid. Remove the bay leaves. Stir in the sugar, lemon juice, and salt. Serve topped with cilantro.

▶ **SERVES 4; 1 1/2 cups (340 g) per serving**

Butternut Apple Ginger Bisque with Yogurt

2 teaspoons (28 ml) canola oil

1 cup (160 g) chopped onion

3 cups (700 ml) water

2 packages (12 ounces [340 g] each) peeled and chopped butternut squash

2 cups (300 g) chopped tart apple, such as Granny Smith or Honeycrisp

1 cup (122 g) frozen sliced carrots

½ teaspoon garlic powder

1 can (13.5 ounces [378 g]) light coconut milk

2 tablespoons (16 g) grated ginger

1½ tablespoons (20 g) sugar, or to taste

1¼ teaspoons salt

¼ teaspoon black pepper, or to taste

1½ cups (345 g) 2% plain Greek yogurt

Make cooking this dish easy on yourself—if fresh peeled squash is not available, just use two 10-ounce (280 g) packages of the frozen variety.

1. Select Browning/Sauté on the pressure cooker. When the pot is hot, add the canola oil. Tilt the pot to lightly coat the bottom. Add the onion and cook for 4 minutes.

2. Add the water, butternut squash, apple, carrots, and garlic powder. Stir to combine. Lock the lid in place and close the seal valve. Press the Cancel button and reset to Manual for 8 minutes.

3. When the cook time ends, use a natural pressure release.

4. When the valve drops, carefully remove the lid. Working in batches, puree the mixture in a blender. Return the pureed mixture to the pot and stir in the coconut milk, ginger, sugar, salt, and pepper.

5. Spoon equal amounts of the bisque into 6 shallow soup bowls, and top each with ¼ cup (60 g) yogurt.

▸ **SERVES 6; 1⅓ cups (303 g) soup plus ¼ cup (60 g) yogurt per serving**

▸ **NUTRITION FACTS**

Amount Per Serving

Calories	180	
Calories from Fat	45	
		% Daily Value
Total Fat	5 g	8%
Saturated Fat	3 g	15%
Trans Fat	0 g	
Cholesterol	5 mg	2%
Sodium	530 mg	22%
Total Carbohydrate	29 g	10%
Dietary Fiber	4 g	16%
Sugars	14 g	
Protein	7 g	
Vitamin A		300%
Vitamin C		45%
Calcium		10%
Iron		6%
Magnesium	46.47 mg	
Potassium	540.29 mg	

Garden Veggie and Two-Cheese Soup

1½ cups (225 g) chopped red bell pepper

¾ cup (75 g) chopped green onion (green and white parts), divided

1 pound (455 g) yellow crookneck squash, coarsely chopped

1 cup (110 g) chopped russet potatoes

¾ cup (175 ml) water

½ teaspoon ground cumin

⅛ teaspoon cayenne pepper

¾ cup (175 ml) 2% milk

½ teaspoon salt

2 ounces (55 g) shredded reduced-fat sharp cheddar cheese

1 ounce (28 g) crumbled reduced-fat blue cheese

▸ **NUTRITION FACTS**

Amount Per Serving

Calories	160	
Calories from Fat	50	
		% Daily Value
Total Fat	6 g	9%
Saturated Fat	3.5 g	18%
Trans Fat	0 g	
Cholesterol	20 mg	7%
Sodium	510 mg	21%
Total Carbohydrate	19 g	6%
Dietary Fiber	4 g	16%
Sugars	8 g	
Protein	10 g	
Vitamin A		45%
Vitamin C		170%
Calcium		25%
Iron		8%
Magnesium	50.63 mg	
Potassium	652.31 mg	

The addition of blue cheese in this soup blends in while bringing out the slight sharpness of the cheddar cheese.

1. Select Browning/Sauté on the pressure cooker. When the pot is hot, coat the pressure cooker pot with cooking spray, then add the bell pepper and ½ cup (50 g) of the green onion; cook for 4 minutes, or until beginning to lightly brown on the edges, stirring frequently.

2. Add the yellow squash, potatoes, water, cumin, and cayenne pepper. Stir to combine. Lock the lid in place and close the seal valve. Press the Cancel button and reset to Manual for 4 minutes.

3. When the cook time ends, use a quick pressure release.

4. When the valve drops, carefully remove the lid. Turn off the pressure cooker. Stir in the milk and salt. Roughly mash the potato mixture with a potato masher or whisk to thicken slightly. Gradually, stir in the cheeses. Let stand, uncovered, for 10 minutes to thicken slightly and allow the cheeses to melt.

5. Serve topped with the remaining ¼ cup (25 g) green onion.

▸ **SERVES 4; 1¼ cups (284 g) per serving**

White Bean Chili with Poblano Topping

2 tablespoons (28 ml) extra virgin olive oil, divided

1½ cups (177 g) chopped poblano pepper

2 cloves garlic, minced

8 ounces (225 g) dried Great Northern beans, rinsed

3 cups (700 ml) water

1½ cups (240 g) chopped onion

2 cans (4 ounces [1152 g] each) chopped green chiles

1 tablespoon (7 g) ground cumin, divided

1 teaspoon dried oregano

3/4 teaspoon salt

2/3 cup (153 g) 2% plain Greek yogurt

This high-fiber, nutrient-dense bowl comes with an added bonus . . . it's even better the next day, or the next, or the next!

1. Select Browning/Sauté on the pressure cooker. When the pot is hot, add 1 tablespoon (15 ml) of the extra virgin olive oil. Tilt the pot to lightly coat the bottom. Add the poblano peppers and cook for 8 minutes or until richly browned, stirring occasionally.

2. Add the remaining 1 tablespoon (15 ml) extra virgin olive oil and the garlic, and cook for 15 seconds, stirring constantly. Reserve 1/3 cup (39 g) of the poblano mixture and set aside in a small bowl.

3. Add the white beans, water, onion, green chiles, 2 teaspoons of the cumin, and oregano. Lock the lid in place and close the seal valve. Press the Cancel button and reset to Manual for 45 minutes.

4. When the cook time ends, use a quick pressure release.

5. When the valve drops, carefully remove the lid and stir in the remaining 1 teaspoon cumin and the salt. Use a potato masher or whisk to break up some of the beans for a thicker consistency. Serve topped with the yogurt and reserved poblano peppers.

▸ **SERVES 6; 1 cup (225 g) soup, 2 tablespoons (30 g) yogurt, and 1 tablespoon (7 g) poblano peppers per serving**

▸ **NUTRITION FACTS**

Amount Per Serving

Calories	270	
Calories from Fat	60	
		% Daily Value
Total Fat	7 g	11%
Saturated Fat	1.5 g	8%
Trans Fat	0 g	
Cholesterol	0 mg	
Sodium	550 mg	23%
Total Carbohydrate	41 g	14%
Dietary Fiber	11 g	44%
Sugars	7 g	
Protein	14 g	
Vitamin A		10%
Vitamin C		220%
Calcium		15%
Iron		20%
Magnesium	103.90 mg	
Potassium	908.35 mg	

Fish Stew with Potatoes and White Wine

1 cup (160 g) chopped onion

1/2 teaspoon garlic powder

1 pound (455 g) red potatoes, coarsely chopped into 3/4-inch (2 cm) cubes

1 can (14.5 ounces [410 g]) no-salt-added diced tomatoes

1 cup (235 ml) dry white wine

1 pound (455 g) cod fillets, cut into 1-inch (2.5 cm) chunks

2 teaspoons seafood seasoning, such as Old Bay

3/4 teaspoon salt

2 tablespoons (28 ml) extra virgin olive oil

1/4 cup (15 g) chopped fresh parsley

Here's cozy, rainy-day favorite, but without the work!

1. Select Browning/Sauté on the pressure cooker. When the pot is hot, coat the pot with cooking spray. Add the onion and cook for 4 minutes.

2. Add the garlic powder, potatoes, tomatoes, and white wine. Stir to combine. Lock the lid in place and close the seal valve. Press the Cancel button and reset to Manual for 3 minutes.

3. When the cook time ends, use a quick pressure release.

4. When the valve drops, carefully remove the lid. Stir in the cod fillets, seafood seasoning, and salt. Lock the lid in place and close the seal valve. Press the Cancel button and reset to Manual for 1 minute.

5. When the cook time ends, use a quick pressure release.

6. When the valve drops, carefully remove the lid. Check the cod fillets for doneness. Stir in the extra virgin olive oil and parsley. Let stand for 10 minutes to allow the flavors to blend.

▶ **SERVES 6; 1 cup (225 g) per serving**

▶ **NUTRITION FACTS**

Amount Per Serving		
Calories	220	
Calories from Fat	50	
		% Daily Value
Total Fat	5 g	8%
Saturated Fat	1 g	5%
Trans Fat	0 g	
Cholesterol	35 mg	12%
Sodium	570 mg	24%
Total Carbohydrate	19 g	6%
Dietary Fiber	2 g	8%
Sugars	5 g	
Protein	16 g	
Vitamin A		15%
Vitamin C		40%
Calcium		4%
Iron		8%
Magnesium	48.67 mg	
Potassium	736.87 mg	

White Wine Mussels with Dipping Bread

48 mussels, (about 2 pounds [900 g] total), scrubbed and debearded

4 shallots, chopped

2 cloves garlic, minced

¼ teaspoon dried thyme leaves

½ cup (120 ml) reduced-sodium chicken broth

½ cup (120 ml) white wine

¼ cup (55 g) light butter with canola oil

1 cup (180 g) diced tomato

Grated zest of 1 lemon

2 tablespoons (8 g) chopped fresh parsley, optional

8 ounces (225 g) multigrain Italian loaf bread, sliced

▸ **NUTRITION FACTS**

Amount Per Serving

Calories	260	
Calories from Fat	70	
		% Daily Value
Total Fat	8 g	12%
Saturated Fat	2 g	10%
Trans Fat	0 g	
Cholesterol	15 mg	5%
Sodium	450 mg	19%
Total Carbohydrate	35 g	12%
Dietary Fiber	5 g	20%
Sugars	7 g	
Protein	11 g	
Vitamin A		15%
Vitamin C		20%
Calcium		8%
Iron		15%
Magnesium	18.35 mg	
Potassium	251.36 mg	

Mussels make such a dramatic presentation for practically no effort! This is one of those dishes you gravitate to on the hottest of summer nights . . . it's quick, it's light, and it's soooooooo easy!

1. Discard any mussels that do not close when tapped against a hard surface or have cracks in them.

2. Press Browning/Sauté on the pressure cooker. When the pot is hot, lightly coat with cooking spray. Add the shallots and cook for 4 minutes, until translucent, stirring frequently. Add the garlic and cook for 15 seconds, stirring constantly. Stir in the thyme, chicken broth, and white wine. Add the mussels. Lock the lid in place and close the seal valve. Press the Cancel button and reset to Manual for 2 minutes.

3. When the cook time ends, use a quick pressure release.

4. When the valve drops, carefully remove the lid. Remove the mussels with a slotted spoon and divide among 4 shallow soup bowls, discarding any mussels that have not opened.

5. Add the butter, tomato, and lemon zest to the liquid in the pot and stir until the butter has melted. Spoon over the mussels in the bowls. Sprinkle with the parsley, if desired. You can cut the lemon into 4 wedges and serve alongside, if desired. Serve with the sliced Italian bread to dip into the flavorful juices in the bowl.

▸ **SERVES 4; 12 mussels (28 g) shelled, ½ cup broth (120 g) and 2 ounces (55 g) bread per serving**

Ale'd Chili with Beans

1 pound (455 g) lean ground beef

1½ cups (177 g) chopped poblano
chile peppers

1 can (14.5 ounces [405 g]) no-salt-added
stewed tomatoes

1 (15-ounce [420 g]) can no-salt-added
dark red kidney beans, rinsed and drained

1½ cups (355 ml) light beer,
such as Miller Lite

3 tablespoons (23 g) chili powder

1 tablespoon (7 g) ground cumin, divided

2 teaspoons dried oregano leaves

1 teaspoon garlic powder

½ cup (8 g) chopped fresh cilantro
or (30 g) parsley

3 tablespoons (45 g) ketchup

1 tablespoon (15 ml) extra virgin olive oil

½ teaspoon salt

This super quick chili tastes like it's been slow simmering for hours. It's great served right away, but you can also freeze leftovers in 1-cup (225 g) portions for a grab-and-go lunch or dinner.

1. Select Browning/Sauté on the pressure cooker. When the pot is hot, lightly coat it with cooking spray. Add the ground beef and cook for 4 minutes or until browned, stirring occasionally. Stir in the poblano peppers, tomatoes, kidney beans, beer, chili powder, 2 teaspoons of cumin, oregano, and garlic powder. Lock the lid in place and close the seal valve. Press the Cancel button and reset to Manual for 15 minutes.

2. When the cook time ends, use a quick pressure release.

3. When the valve drops, carefully remove the lid. Stir in the cilantro, ketchup, extra virgin olive oil, salt, and remaining 1 teaspoon cumin.

▸ **SERVES 6; About 1 cup (255 g) per serving**

▸ **NUTRITION FACTS**

Amount Per Serving

Calories	240	
Calories from Fat	80	

		% Daily Value
Total Fat	9 g	14%
Saturated Fat	3 g	15%
Trans Fat	0 g	
Cholesterol	45 mg	15%
Sodium	460 mg	19%
Total Carbohydrate	20 g	7%
Dietary Fiber	7 g	28%
Sugars	7 g	
Protein	21 g	

Vitamin A		40%
Vitamin C		160%
Calcium		8%
Iron		15%
Magnesium	31.40 mg	
Potassium	490.30 mg	

Cook's Note:
For a deeper chili taste, stir in ½ to 1 teaspoon additional ground cumin at the end.

Brothy Chicken, Artichoke, and Kale Bowls

4 boneless, skinless (4 ounces [112 g] each) chicken thighs

1 package (9 ounces [252 g]) frozen artichoke hearts

1 cup (235 ml) water

½ teaspoon dried rosemary

1 package (8 ounces [227 g]) baby kale mix

1 tablespoon (15 ml) extra virgin olive oil

½ teaspoon salt

2 ounces (55 g) shredded Italian five-cheese blend

Black pepper

Have you ever tried cooking with frozen artichokes—not the canned or the marinated version, but the frozen variety? If not, this is the perfect recipe to experiment with, and then you'll be hooked. Frozen artichokes make a great new addition to your own list of healthy ingredients. It adds a new avenue of flavor, texture, and nutrients, including a good source of fiber—and all without added sodium or fat!

1. Place the chicken, artichokes, water, and rosemary in the pressure cooker pot. Lock the lid in place and close the seal valve. Press the Cancel button and reset to Manual for 6 minutes.

2. When the cook time ends, do a 5-minute natural release, then a quick pressure release.

3. When the valve drops, carefully remove the lid. Check the chicken for doneness. Remove chicken and let stand on a cutting board for 5 minutes before shredding.

Amount Per Serving		
Calories	250	
Calories from Fat	100	
		% Daily Value
Total Fat	11 g	17%
Saturated Fat	3.5 g	18%
Trans Fat	0 g	
Cholesterol	115 mg	38%
Sodium	570 mg	24%
Total Carbohydrate	7 g	2%
Dietary Fiber	4 g	16%
Sugars	0 g	
Protein	30 g	
Vitamin A		50%
Vitamin C		30%
Calcium		30%
Iron		10%
Magnesium	43.31 mg	
Potassium	712.84 mg	

4. Meanwhile, press the Cancel button. Select Browning/ Sauté. Bring the artichoke mixture to a boil. Stir in the kale mix, extra virgin olive oil, and salt and cook until just wilted, about 1 minute, stirring constantly.

5. Divide the artichoke mixture among 4 shallow soup bowls. Top with the shredded chicken, shredded cheese, and black pepper.

▸ **SERVES 4; 1 cup (177 g) kale mixture, 3 ounces (85 g) chicken, and 1/2 ounce (15 g) cheese per serving**

Chipotle Pork, Hominy, and Avocado Stew

2 tablespoons (30 ml) extra virgin olive oil, divided

1 pound (454 g) trimmed boneless pork shoulder steak, cut into 1-inch (2.5 cm) cubes

1 can (14.5 ounces [410 g]) no-salt-added stewed tomatoes

1 can (15.5 ounces [438 g]) yellow or white hominy, rinsed and drained

2 cans (4 ounces [112 g] each) chopped green chiles

1 chipotle chile in adobo sauce, finely chopped

1 tablespoon (4 g) sodium-free granulated chicken bouillon

2 teaspoons ground cumin

1 tablespoon (13 g) sugar

3/4 teaspoon salt

2 avocados, peeled, pitted, and chopped

1/2 cup (58 g) finely chopped radish

1/2 cup (8 g) chopped fresh cilantro, optional

1 lime, cut into 6 wedges

You've heard of topping soups and stews with avocado, but have you ever tried adding it to the soup or stew? Just stir it in gently and it will hold its shape to some degree and add a bit of creaminess to the dish.

1. Select Browning/Sauté on the pressure cooker. When the pot is hot, add 1 tablespoon (15 ml) of extra virgin olive oil. Tilt the pot to lightly coat the bottom. Add the pork in a single layer and cook for 5 minutes; do not stir. Add the tomatoes, hominy, green chiles, chipotle, chicken, bouillon, and cumin. Sprinkle the sugar on top, but do not stir. Lock the lid in place and close the seal valve. Press the Cancel button, then reset to Manual for 30 minutes.

2. When the cook time ends, use a natural pressure release.

Amount Per Serving		
Calories	320	
Calories from Fat	180	
		% Daily Value
Total Fat	20 g	31%
Saturated Fat	5 g	25%
Trans Fat	0 g	
Cholesterol	45 mg	15%
Sodium	570 mg	24%
Total Carbohydrate	20 g	7%
Dietary Fiber	6 g	24%
Sugars	8 g	
Protein	14 g	
Vitamin A		10%
Vitamin C		40%
Calcium		4%
Iron		15%
Magnesium	32.92 mg	
Potassium	489.79 mg	

3. When the valve drops, carefully remove the lid. Check the pork for doneness. Stir in the remaining 1 tablespoon (15 ml) extra virgin olive oil and the salt. Gently stir in the avocado.

4. Divide the stew among 6 shallow bowls. Top with the radish and cilantro, if desired. Serve with the lime wedges alongside.

▸ **SERVES 6; 1⅓ cups (264 g) per serving**

Simple Home-Style Beef Stew

2 tablespoons (28 ml) canola oil

1½ pounds (680 g) lean beef stew meat

3 ribs celery, cut into 2-inch (5 cm) pieces

2 medium onions (8 ounces [225 g] total), cut into 8 wedges each

1 cup (235 ml) water

1 bay leaf

1 teaspoon garlic powder

1 teaspoon instant coffee granules

2 tablespoons (28 ml) Worcestershire sauce

1½ pounds (680 g) carrots, cut into 2-inch (5 cm) pieces

2 pounds (900 g) petite potatoes, halved

¾ teaspoon salt

½ teaspoon black pepper

This classic, straightforward stew is one that will please grown-ups and kids alike. The addition of coffee granules is the secret ingredient that helps bring out the deep flavor of the beef. No one will ever know!

1. Select Browning/Sauté on the pressure cooker. When the pot is hot, add canola oil and tilt the pot to coat the bottom lightly. Pat the beef dry with paper towels. Add half of the beef in a single layer and brown on one side for 5 minutes; do not turn. Transfer the beef to a plate and repeat with the remaining beef.

2. Stir in the reserved beef, celery, onions, water, bay leaf, garlic powder, and coffee granules. Spoon the Worcestershire sauce evenly over all, but do not stir. Top with the carrots and potatoes. Lock the lid in place and close the seal valve. Press the Cancel button and reset to Manual for 35 minutes.

3. When the cook time ends, use a quick pressure release.

Amount Per Serving

Calories	280	
Calories from Fat	90	
		% Daily Value
Total Fat	10 g	15%
Saturated Fat	2.5 g	13%
Trans Fat	0 g	
Cholesterol	55 mg	18%
Sodium	470 mg	20%
Total Carbohydrate	30 g	10%
Dietary Fiber	5 g	20%
Sugars	7 g	
Protein	19 g	
Vitamin A		290%
Vitamin C		30%
Calcium		6%
Iron		20%
Magnesium	50.64 mg	
Potassium	1054.84 mg	

4. When the valve drops, carefully remove the lid. Check the beef for doneness. Transfer the meat and vegetables to a large shallow bowl, such as a pasta bowl. Cover to keep warm.

5. Press the Cancel button. Select Browning/Sauté. Stir in the salt and pepper. Bring the liquid in the pressure cooker pot to a boil and boil for 5 minutes or until the liquid is reduced to 2 cups (475 ml). Remove the bay leaf. Serve the stew in shallow bowls to contain the au jus.

▸ **SERVES 8; 1½ cups (227 g) beef and vegetable mixture plus ¼ cup (60 ml) au jus per serving**

Portobello and Sherry Beef Stew

2 tablespoons (28 ml) extra virgin olive oil, divided

12 ounces (340 g) lean beef stew meat

12 ounces (340 g) sliced portobello mushrooms

2 medium onions, cut into 8 wedges each (about 8 ounces [225 g] total)

2 medium carrots, cut into 2-inch (5 cm) pieces (about 6 ounces [170 g] total)

1/3 cup (80 ml) water

3 tablespoons (45 ml) reduced-sodium soy sauce

1/3 cup (80 ml) dry sherry or Madeira wine

2 teaspoons instant coffee granules

2 teaspoons dried oregano

2 teaspoons Worcestershire sauce

1/2 teaspoon black pepper

2 teaspoons sugar

Not a sherry or Madeira drinker? No worries: you can purchase very small bottles to use in this delicious stew. You can also use sherry or Madeira in small amounts in other dishes, such as chicken or pork stew, to add a new dimension of flavor.

1. Select Browning/Sauté on the pressure cooker. When the pot is hot, add 1 tablespoon (15 ml) of extra virgin olive oil and tilt the pot to lightly coat the bottom. Add the beef in a single layer and cook for 5 minutes; do not stir.

2. Add the mushrooms, onions, carrots, water, soy sauce, sherry, coffee granules, oregano, Worcestershire sauce, and pepper. Lock the lid in place and close the seal valve. Press the Cancel button, then reset to Manual for 25 minutes.

Cook's Note:
For a variation, serve over riced cauliflower or zucchini spirals.

▶ NUTRITION FACTS

Amount Per Serving

Calories	280	
Calories from Fat	120	

		% Daily Value
Total Fat	13 g	20%
Saturated Fat	3.5 g	18%
Trans Fat	0 g	
Cholesterol	55 mg	18%
Sodium	530 mg	22%
Total Carbohydrate	17 g	6%
Dietary Fiber	3 g	12%
Sugars	9 g	
Protein	20 g	

Vitamin A		140%
Vitamin C		10%
Calcium		4%
Iron		15%
Magnesium	36.26 mg	
Potassium	729.93mg	

3. When the cook time ends, use a natural pressure release for 10 minutes, then a quick pressure release.

4. When the valve drops, carefully remove the lid. Check the beef for doneness. Add the sugar and remaining 1 tablespoon (15 ml) extra virgin olive oil to the beef mixture.

5. Press the Cancel button and then select Browning/ Sauté. Bring the liquid in the pot to a boil and boil for 10 minutes or until slightly thickened. Serve in shallow bowls.

▶ **SERVES 4; 1 cup (213 g) per serving**

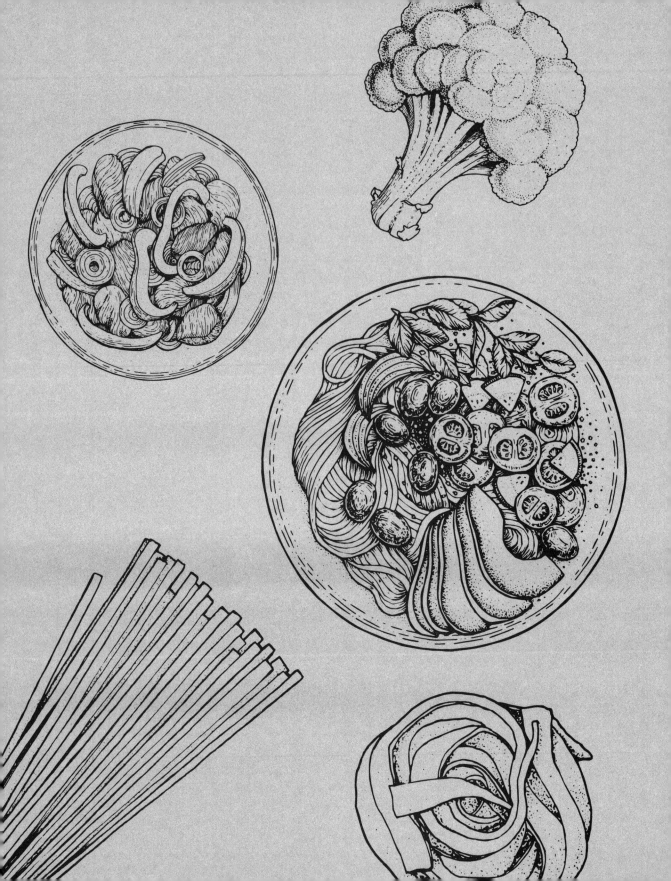

4

Pasta and Egg Noodle Dinners

Cheddar Broccoli Almond Pasta

6 ounces (170 g) uncooked whole-grain rotini pasta

3 cups (700 ml) water

2 cups (142 g) broccoli florets

½ cup (50 g) chopped green onion

⅓ cup (80 ml) 2% milk

2 ounces (55 g) reduced-fat cream cheese, cut into small cubes

3 ounces (85 g) shredded reduced-fat sharp cheddar cheese

2 ounces (55 g) sliced almonds

¼ teaspoon plus ⅛ teaspoon salt, divided

⅛ teaspoon cayenne pepper

Cook the pasta for 4 minutes, add the broccoli for 1 minute, and then toss the rest in . . . DONE!

1. Combine the pasta and water in the pressure cooker pot. Lock the lid in place and close the seal valve. Press the Manual button for 4 minutes.

2. When the cook time ends, use a quick pressure release.

3. When the valve drops, carefully remove the lid. Stir in the broccoli. Lock the lid in place and close the seal valve. Press the Cancel button and reset to Manual for 1 minute.

▸ NUTRITION FACTS

Amount Per Serving

Calories	350	
Calories from Fat	150	

		% Daily Value
Total Fat	17 g	26%
Saturated Fat	6 g	30%
Trans Fat	0 g	
Cholesterol	25 mg	8%
Sodium	470 mg	20%
Total Carbohydrate	37 g	12%
Dietary Fiber	7 g	28%
Sugars	4 g	
Protein	18 g	

Vitamin A		30%
Vitamin C		60%
Calcium		25%
Iron		10%
Magnesium	55.20 mg	
Potassium	287.37 mg	

4. When the cook time ends, use a quick pressure release.

5. Drain the pasta mixture in a colander and return to the pot. Gently stir in the green onion, milk, cream cheese, two-thirds of the cheddar cheese, almonds, ¼ teaspoon of the salt, and cayenne pepper. Sprinkle with the remaining ⅛ teaspoon salt and cheddar cheese.

▸ **SERVES 4; 1½ cups (227 g) per serving**

Chicken, Pasta, and Veggie Toss with Feta

12 ounces (340 g) boneless, skinless chicken thighs

3 cups (700 ml) water

2 teaspoons dried Italian seasoning, divided

4 ounces (115 g) whole-grain rotini or penne

1 red bell pepper, cored and cut into thin strips

1 medium zucchini, sliced

3 cups (90 g) baby spinach

1 clove garlic, minced

1 tablespoon (15 ml) extra virgin olive oil

1/8 teaspoon salt

3 ounces (85 g) crumbled reduced-fat feta cheese

This is a "one-pot-cooks-all" dish, cooked in simple stages: add the chicken, then the pasta, and then, at the very end, add the veggies . . . and there's only one pot to clean!

1. Combine the chicken, water, and 1 teaspoon of Italian seasoning in the pressure cooker pot. Lock the lid in place and close the seal valve. Press the Manual button for 15 minutes.

2. When the cook time ends, use a quick pressure release.

3. When the valve drops, carefully remove the lid. Check teh chicken for doneness. Transfer the chicken to a cutting board and let stand for 5 minutes before coarsely shredding.

4. Meanwhile, add the pasta to the pot, making sure the pasta is completely covered with liquid. Lock the lid in place and close the seal valve. Press the Cancel button, then reset to Manual for 3 minutes.

5. When the cook time ends, use a quick pressure release.

Amount Per Serving

Calories	310
Calories from Fat	120

		% Daily Value
Total Fat	13 g	20%
Saturated Fat	4 g	20%
Trans Fat	0 g	
Cholesterol	65 mg	22%
Sodium	430 mg	18%
Total Carbohydrate	24 g	8%
Dietary Fiber	4 g	16%
Sugars	2 g	
Protein	27 g	

Vitamin A	50%
Vitamin C	100%
Calcium	10%
Iron	15%
Magnesium	43.87 mg
Potassium	376.15 mg

6. When the valve drops, carefully remove the lid. Stir in the bell pepper and zucchini. Lock the lid in place and close the seal valve. Press the Cancel button and reset to Manual for 1 minute.

7. When the cook time ends, use a quick pressure release.

8. When the valve drops, carefully remove the lid. Drain the pasta well. Return the drained pasta and vegetable mixture to the pressure cooker pot and add the shredded chicken, spinach, garlic, extra virgin olive oil, salt, and remaining 1 teaspoon Italian seasoning. Toss until the spinach is slightly wilted. Sprinkle with crumbled feta cheese.

▶ **SERVES 4; 1½ cups (227 g) per serving**

Chicken and Pasta with White Wine and Olives

12 ounces (340 g) boneless, skinless chicken thighs, cut into bite-size pieces

3 ounces (85 g) whole-grain rotini or penne

1 can (14.5 ounces [410 g]) no-salt-added diced tomatoes

1 cup (235 ml) water

1 cup (235 ml) dry white wine

½ teaspoon dried rosemary

⅛ teaspoon crushed red pepper flakes, optional

16 kalamata olives, pitted and coarsely chopped

2 cups (60 g) baby spinach

2 tablespoons (28 ml) extra virgin olive oil

¼ teaspoon salt

Here's a dish that has "all day" simmering flavors in a bowl that's ready in 15 minutes!

1. Combine the chicken, pasta, tomatoes, water, white wine, rosemary, and red pepper flakes (if using) in the pressure cooker pot. Lock the lid in place and close the seal valve. Press the Manual button for 4 minutes.

2. When the cook time ends, use a natural pressure release for 5 minutes, then a quick pressure release.

Amount Per Serving

Calories	370	
Calories from Fat	160	
		% Daily Value
Total Fat	18 g	28%
Saturated Fat	3 g	15%
Trans Fat	0 g	
Cholesterol	55 mg	18%
Sodium	460 mg	19%
Total Carbohydrate	23 g	8%
Dietary Fiber	3 g	12%
Sugars	4 g	
Protein	20 g	
Vitamin A		30%
Vitamin C		35%
Calcium		6%
Iron		15%
Magnesium	27.67mg	
Potassium	156.95 mg	

3. When the valve drops, carefully remove the lid. Check the chicken for doneness. Discard 1 cup (235 ml) of the liquid. Stir in the olives, spinach, extra virgin olive oil, and salt.

4. Press the Cancel button and reset to Browning/Sauté. Bring to a boil and cook for 5 minutes to thicken slightly and allow the flavors to blend. Serve in shallow bowls to contain the flavorful juices.

▶ **SERVES 4; 1½ cups (227 g) per serving**

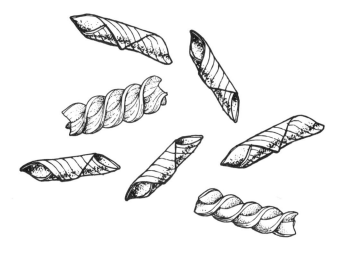

Veggie-Packed Chicken and Noodles

1 pound (455 g) boneless, skinless chicken breast, cut into bite-size pieces

12 ounces (340 g) frozen mixed vegetables

2 cups (168 g) frozen peppers and onions

4 ounces (115 g) uncooked no-yolk egg noodles

2 cups (475 ml) water

1 tablespoon (4 g) sodium-free granulated chicken bouillon

1 teaspoon dried thyme

1 teaspoon garlic powder

¼ cup (60 ml) 2% milk

1 ounce (28 g) crumbled reduced-fat blue cheese

2 tablespoons (28 g) light butter with canola oil

1 teaspoon salt

¼ teaspoon black pepper

This "stir and serve" recipe will bring comfort in every bite, and it's even better the next day. The small amount of blue cheese adds a bit of punch, but no one will ever know it's in the dish.

1. Combine the chicken, mixed vegetables, peppers and onions, egg noodles, water, chicken bouillon granules, thyme, and garlic powder in the pressure cooker pot. Lock the lid in place and close the seal valve. Press the Manual button for 5 minutes.

2. When the cook time ends, use a quick pressure release.

Amount Per Serving

Calories	260	
Calories from Fat	50	
		% Daily Value
Total Fat	6 g	9%
Saturated Fat	2.5 g	13%
Trans Fat	0 g	
Cholesterol	65 mg	22%
Sodium	550 mg	23%
Total Carbohydrate	26 g	9%
Dietary Fiber	2 g	8%
Sugars	6 g	
Protein	23 g	
Vitamin A		90%
Vitamin C		0%
Calcium		6%
Iron		4%
Magnesium	33.70 mg	
Potassium	425.13 mg	

3. When the valve drops, carefully remove the lid. Check the chicken for doneness. Turn off the pressure cooker. Stir in the milk, blue cheese, butter, salt, and pepper. Let stand, uncovered, for 10 minutes to allow the flavors to blend. Serve in shallow bowls to contain the flavorful sauce.

▸ **SERVES 6; 1¹/₃ cups (209 g) per serving**

Beef, Red Wine, and Rotini

1 tablespoon (15 ml) canola oil

12 ounces (340 g) trimmed lean boneless chuck roast, cut into 1-inch (2.5 cm) pieces

3 cups (252 g) frozen peppers and onions

1 package (8 ounces [225 g]) sliced baby portobello mushrooms

1 cup (235 ml) red wine

2 teaspoons sodium-free granulated beef bouillon

2 teaspoons dried Italian seasoning

3 ounces (84 g) uncooked whole-grain rotini pasta

1/3 cup (80 g) ketchup

1 tablespoon (15 ml) balsamic vinegar

1/2 teaspoon salt

Portobello mushrooms have a firmer texture and more flavor than ordinary white mushrooms, providing a "meatier" feel to the dish.

1. Select Browning/Sauté on the pressure cooker. When the pot is hot, add the canola oil and tilt the pot to coat the bottom lightly. Add the beef and cook without stirring for 3 minutes.

2. Stir in the peppers and onions, mushrooms, red wine, beef bouillon granules, and Italian seasoning. Lock the lid in place and close the seal valve. Press the Cancel button, then reset to Manual for 20 minutes.

3. When the cook time ends, use a quick pressure release.

4. When the valve drops, carefully remove the lid. Check the beef for doneness. Stir in the pasta. Close the lid securely and close the seal valve. Press the Cancel button and reset to Manual for 4 minutes.

▸ NUTRITION FACTS

Amount Per Serving

Calories	310	
Calories from Fat	70	

		% Daily Value
Total Fat	8 g	12%
Saturated Fat	1.5 g	8%
Trans Fat	0 g	
Cholesterol	35 mg	12%
Sodium	540 mg	23%
Total Carbohydrate	29 g	10%
Dietary Fiber	4 g	16%
Sugars	10 g	
Protein	22 g	

Vitamin A		15%
Vitamin C		70%
Calcium		2%
Iron		15%
Magnesium	27.43 mg	
Potassium	478.21 mg	

5. When the cook time ends, use a quick pressure release.

6. When the valve drops, carefully remove the lid. Stir in the ketchup, balsamic vinegar, and salt. Press the Cancel button and reset to Browning/Sauté. Bring to a boil and cook for 3 minutes to thicken slightly and allow the flavors to blend.

▸ **SERVES 4; 1 cup (248 g) per serving**

Spaghetti Pot Pasta with Red Wine

12 ounces (340 g) lean ground beef

4 ounces (115 g) uncooked whole-grain spaghetti, broken into thirds

2 large red bell peppers, cored and coarsely chopped

4 ounces (115 g) sliced mushrooms

1½ cups (355 ml) low-sodium pasta sauce, such as Prego Heart Smart

3/4 cup (175 ml) red wine (or 3/4 cup [175 ml] water and 1 teaspoon sodium-free granulated beef bouillon)

1 tablespoon (16 g) tomato paste

2 teaspoons dried Italian seasoning

1/8 teaspoon crushed red pepper flakes, optional

1½ teaspoons sugar

1/4 teaspoon salt

4 teaspoons (7 g) grated Parmesan cheese

Generally speaking, when adding red wine to spaghetti, you usually use ¼ to ⅓ cup (60 to 80 ml) for this amount of pasta and beef. But in this recipe, it's almost tripled, turning a simple spaghetti dish into a great tasting sensation brimming with a heady aroma.

1. Select Browning/Sauté on the pressure cooker. When the pot is hot, coat with cooking spray. Cook the beef for 4 minutes or until beginning to brown, stirring occasionally.

2. Stir in the pasta, bell peppers, mushrooms, pasta sauce, red wine, tomato paste, Italian seasoning, and red pepper flakes (if using). Make sure the pasta is submerged by pressing down lightly with back of a spoon or a spatula. Lock the lid in place and close the seal valve. Press the Manual button for 5 minutes.

Cook's Note:

There will be brown bits on the bottom of the pot, but after 3 minutes of standing, the brown bits will be released and incorporated with the other ingredients to provide additional flavor.

▶ NUTRITION FACTS

Amount Per Serving

Calories	350
Calories from Fat	80

		% Daily Value
Total Fat	9 g	14%
Saturated Fat	3.5 g	18%
Trans Fat	0 g	
Cholesterol	55 mg	18%
Sodium	520 mg	22%
Total Carbohydrate	38 g	13%
Dietary Fiber	7 g	28%
Sugars	14 g	
Protein	26 g	

Vitamin A		60%
Vitamin C		180%
Calcium		6%
Iron		10%
Magnesium	17.79 mg	
Potassium	606.47 mg	

3. When the cook time ends, use a quick pressure release.

4. When the valve drops, carefully remove the lid. Check the beef for doneness. Turn off the pressure cooker. Stir in the sugar and salt. Cover with the lid, but do not lock. Let stand for 3 minutes to thicken slightly and allow the flavors to blend. Serve topped with the Parmesan cheese.

▶ **SERVES 4; 1½ cups (319 g) per serving**

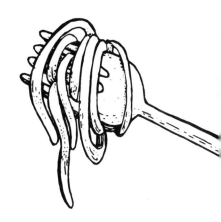

5

Grain, Rice, and Bean Dinners

Wild Rice Pilaf, Dried Apricots, and Edamame

1½ ounces (42 g) unsalted hulled sunflower seeds

⅔ cup (107 g) wild rice

⅓ cup (63 g) brown rice

3 cups (700 ml) water

8 ounces (225 g) shelled edamame

¼ cup (25 g) chopped green onion

½ cup (65 g) dried apricots, chopped

½ teaspoon dried sage

¼ teaspoon crushed red pepper flakes

¾ teaspoon salt

1 tablespoon (15 ml) sesame oil

Wild rice and brown rice take the same amount of time in a pressure cooker, so why not have both in one meal, giving more texture and eye appeal to your favorite rice-based dishes.

1. Select Browning/Sauté on the pressure cooker. When the pot is hot, add the sunflower seeds to the pot and cook for 4 minutes or until lightly browned, stirring occasionally. Transfer to a plate and set aside.

2. Combine the wild rice, brown rice, and water in the pressure cooker pot. Lock the lid in place and close the seal valve. Press the Cancel button and reset to Manual for 20 minutes.

Cook's Note:
For a slightly sweeter pilaf, add 1 tablespoon (20 g) honey when adding the remaining ingredients.

▸ NUTRITION FACTS

Amount Per Serving

Calories	360
Calories from Fat	110

		% Daily Value
Total Fat	12 g	18%
Saturated Fat	1 g	5%
Trans Fat	0 g	
Cholesterol	0 mg	
Sodium	470 mg	20%
Total Carbohydrate	52 g	17%
Dietary Fiber	8 g	32%
Sugars	11 g	
Protein	14 g	

Vitamin A		20%
Vitamin C		10%
Calcium		8%
Iron		15%
Magnesium	88.33 mg	
Potassium	432.85 mg	

3. When the cook time ends, use a quick pressure release.

4. When the valve drops, carefully remove the lid. Stir in the edamame and let stand for 1 minute to heat through. Drain the rice mixture in a fine-mesh sieve. Return it to the pot and stir in the toasted sunflower seeds, green onion, apricots, sage, red pepper flakes, salt, and sesame oil.

▸ **SERVES 4; 1¼ cups (199 g) per serving**

Multi-Pepper Black Beans and Rice

3 ounces (85 g) dried black beans, rinsed

3 cups (252 g) frozen peppers and onions

1 jalapeño pepper, seeded and chopped

2 cups (475 ml) water

½ teaspoon garlic powder

2 dried bay leaves

¼ cup (4 g) chopped fresh cilantro

1 tablespoon (15 ml) extra virgin olive oil

1 teaspoon ground cumin

¾ teaspoon salt

1 pouch (8.8 ounces [246 g]) brown rice, such as Ready Rice

¾ cup (180 g) reduced-fat sour cream

1 cup (180 g) chopped tomatoes

1 lime, cut into 4 wedges, optional

This easy-to-fix bowl of comfort is just what's needed after a busy, exhausting day—and it's practically chop-free!

1. Combine the black beans, peppers and onions, jalapeño, water, garlic powder, and bay leaves in the pressure cooker pot. Lock the lid in place and close the seal valve. Press the Manual button for 25 minutes.

2. When the cook time ends, use a quick pressure release.

Amount Per Serving		
Calories	310	
Calories from Fat	70	
		% Daily Value
Total Fat	8 g	12%
Saturated Fat	3 g	15%
Trans Fat	0 g	
Cholesterol	15 mg	5%
Sodium	500 mg	21%
Total Carbohydrate	45 g	15%
Dietary Fiber	8 g	32%
Sugars	10 g	
Protein	10 g	
Vitamin A		30%
Vitamin C		20%
Calcium		10%
Iron		10%
Magnesium	5.75 mg	
Potassium	439.56 mg	

3. When the valve drops, carefully remove the lid. Turn off the heat. Drain the beans, reserving ½ cup (120 ml) of the liquid. Return the beans to the pot with the reserved liquid and stir in the cilantro, extra virgin olive oil, cumin, and salt. Remove the bay leaves.

4. Prepare the rice according to the package directions. Serve the beans over the rice and top with the sour cream and chopped tomatoes. Serve with the lime wedges alongside, if desired.

▸ **SERVES 4; ½ cup (115 g) beans, ½ cup (70 g) rice, and 3 tablespoons (45 g) sour cream per serving**

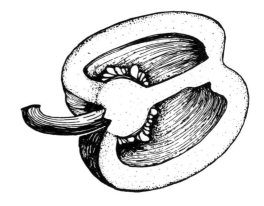

Lentils, Tomatoes, and Feta

3/4 cup (144 g) dried brown lentils, rinsed and drained

2 cups (168 g) frozen peppers and onions

2 cups (244 g) frozen sliced carrots

1 cup (100 g) chopped celery

1 can (14.5 ounces [410 g]) no-salt-added diced tomatoes

1 cup (235 ml) water

1½ teaspoons smoked paprika

½ teaspoon ground cumin

¼ cup (4 g) chopped fresh cilantro or (15 g) parsley

1 tablespoon (15 ml) extra virgin olive oil

3/4 teaspoon salt

3 ounces (85 g) crumbled reduced-fat feta cheese

Combine, seal, and sprinkle with cheese . . . that's all you do.

1. Combine the lentils, peppers and onions, carrots, celery, tomatoes, water, smoked paprika, and cumin in the pressure cooker pot. Lock the lid in place and close the seal valve. Press the Manual button for 7 minutes.

2. When the cook time ends, use a quick pressure release.

3. When the valve drops, carefully remove the lid. Stir in the cilantro, extra virgin olive oil, and salt. Let stand for 5 minutes to allow the flavors to blend. Serve the lentil mixture topped with the crumbled feta cheese.

▸ **SERVES 6; 1 cup (225 g) per serving**

▸ **NUTRITION FACTS**

Amount Per Serving

Calories	180	
Calories from Fat	45	
		% Daily Value
Total Fat	4.5 g	7%
Saturated Fat	1.5 g	8%
Trans Fat	0 g	
Cholesterol	5 mg	2%
Sodium	530 mg	22%
Total Carbohydrate	24 g	8%
Dietary Fiber	5 g	20%
Sugars	6 g	
Protein	10 g	
Vitamin A		140%
Vitamin C		25%
Calcium		8%
Iron		10%
Magnesium	16.41 mg	
Potassium	262.81 mg	

Shrimp and Buckwheat Pilaf

2 tablespoons (28 ml) extra virgin olive oil, divided

12 ounces (340 g) peeled raw shrimp

1 clove garlic, minced

1 3/4 cups (410 ml) water

1 cup (184 g) buckwheat groats, rinsed and drained

1/3 cup (18 g) sliced sun-dried tomatoes (NOT in oil)

2 teaspoons dried oregano

1/8 teaspoon crushed red pepper flakes

16 kalamata olives, pitted and coarsely chopped

1/4 teaspoon salt

The secret to cooking buckwheat is not to cook it too long. If you do, you'll have mushy results. You want it to provide a bit of texture to the dish. Buckwheat groats are sold in major grocery stores and health food stores.

1. Select Browning/Sauté on the pressure cooker. When the pot is hot, add 1 tablespoon (15 ml) of extra virgin olive oil. Tilt the pot to lightly coat the bottom. Add the shrimp and cook for 4 minutes or until pink on the outside and opaque in the center. Add the garlic and cook for 30 seconds, stirring constantly. Transfer to a plate and set aside.

2. Add the water, buckwheat groats, sun-dried tomatoes, oregano, and red pepper flakes to the pressure cooker pot. Lock the lid in place and close the seal valve. Press the Manual button for 2 minutes.

3. When the cook time ends, use a natural pressure release for 5 minutes, then a quick pressure release.

4. When the valve drops, carefully remove the lid. Stir in the reserved shrimp, olives, salt, and remaining 1 tablespoon (15 ml) extra virgin olive oil. Cover, do not lock, and let stand for 3 minutes to heat the shrimp through and allow the flavors to blend.

▶ **SERVES 4; 1 cup (225 g) per serving**

▶ **NUTRITION FACTS**

Amount Per Serving

Calories	320	
Calories from Fat	120	
		% Daily Value
Total Fat	13 g	20%
Saturated Fat	2 g	10%
Trans Fat	0 g	
Cholesterol	105 mg	35%
Sodium	530 mg	22%
Total Carbohydrate	35 g	12%
Dietary Fiber	5 g	20%
Sugars	2 g	
Protein	17 g	
Vitamin A		0%
Vitamin C		2%
Calcium		6%
Iron		10%
Magnesium	99.34 mg	
Potassium	285.44 mg	

Seafood Biryani with Turmeric and Ginger

2 tablespoons (28 ml) canola oil, divided

8 ounces (225 g) raw peeled shrimp

8 ounces (225 g) cod fillets, cut into
  1-inch (2.5 cm) pieces

1½ cups (240 g) chopped onion

2 teaspoons garam masala, store-bought
  or homemade (recipe follows)

¼ teaspoon ground turmeric

1 cup (150 g) chopped red bell pepper

½ cup (75 g) golden raisins

½ cup (90 g) basmati rice

½ cup (87 g) quinoa

1½ cups (355 ml) water

1 tablespoon (8 g) grated fresh ginger

¾ teaspoon salt

Black pepper, optional

Shrimp dishes can be expensive, so why not mix it up a bit with other seafood not only to cut the cost but also to add interest? Garam masala is a blend of herbs and spices. One way to use the spice blend is to purchase it and split it with a friend or make your own (see below). Either way, add this to your pantry shelf and open a new world of flavor.

1. Select Browning/Sauté on the pressure cooker. When the pot is hot, add 1 tablespoon (15 ml) of canola oil to the pot. Tilt the pot to coat the bottom lightly. Add the shrimp and cook for 4 minutes, or until opaque in the center. Transfer to a plate and set aside. Add the cod fillets and cook until opaque inside and outside. Set aside with the shrimp.

2. Add the remaining 1 tablespoon (15 ml) canola oil to the pressure cooker pot. Add the onion and cook for 4 minutes or until golden brown. Stir in the garam masala and turmeric; cook, stirring constantly, for 15 seconds or until fragrant. Stir in the bell pepper, golden raisins, basmati rice, quinoa, and water, scraping to remove the browned bits from the bottom of the pan. Lock the lid in place and close the seal valve. Press the Cancel button and reset to Manual for 4 minutes.

Amount Per Serving

Calories	380	
Calories from Fat	90	
		% Daily Value
Total Fat	10 g	15%
Saturated Fat	0.5 g	3%
Trans Fat	0 g	
Cholesterol	95 mg	32%
Sodium	560 mg	23%
Total Carbohydrate	49 g	16%
Dietary Fiber	7 g	28%
Sugars	15 g	
Protein	23 g	
Vitamin A		25%
Vitamin C		90%
Calcium		8%
Iron		10%
Magnesium	53.31 mg	
Potassium	628.56 mg	

3. When the cook time ends, use a quick pressure release.

4. When the valve drops, carefully remove the lid. Stir in the ginger, reserved seafood, and salt. Cover with the lid (do not lock) and let stand for 2 minutes to heat through and allow the flavors to blend. Sprinkle with black pepper, if desired.

▶ **SERVES 4; 1½ cups (291 g) per serving**

Cook's Note:

You'll find garam masala in your spice aisle, or if you prefer, you can combine these ingredients to create a similar flavor:

Homemade Garam Masala

1½ teaspoons ground cumin

¼ teaspoon ground cinnamon

⅛ teaspoon ground turmeric

⅛ teaspoon ground nutmeg

⅛ teaspoon cayenne pepper

⅛ teaspoon ground allspice

Herbed White Beans and Ham Hocks

8 ounces (225 g) dried large white beans, rinsed and drained

3 cups (700 ml) water

1½ teaspoons dried thyme leaves

1 dried bay leaf

1 teaspoon garlic powder

2 smoked ham hocks (about 1 pound [455 g] total)

2 cups (180 g) chopped green cabbage

2 cups (260 g) chopped carrot

1½ cups (240 g) chopped onion

1 teaspoon salt

Hot sauce, for serving

This is a true taste of the South with all the "back burner" tenderness in a fraction of the time.

1. Combine the white beans, water, thyme, bay leaf, and garlic powder in the pressure cooker pot. Top with the ham hocks, cabbage, carrots, and onion. Lock the lid in place and close the seal valve. Press the Manual button for 25 minutes.

2. When the cook time ends, use a natural pressure release.

Amount Per Serving			
Calories	200		
Calories from Fat	30		
			% Daily Value
Total Fat	3 g		5%
Saturated Fat	1 g		5%
Trans Fat	0 g		
Cholesterol	15 mg		5%
Sodium	490 mg		20%
Total Carbohydrate	32 g		11%
Dietary Fiber	8 g		32%
Sugars	5 g		
Protein	13 g		
Vitamin A			140%
Vitamin C			25%
Calcium			10%
Iron			20%
Magnesium	71.34 mg		
Potassium	789.82 mg		

3. When the valve drops, carefully remove the lid. Transfer the ham hocks and place on a cutting board.

4. When the ham hocks are cool enough to handle, remove the meat from the bones; discard bones and any fat and gristle. Shred the ham into bite-size pieces. Stir ham and salt into the bean mixture; you may whisk briskly to break up some of the beans to thicken mixture slightly, if desired. Remove the bay leaf. Drizzle hot sauce evenly over all.

▸ **SERVES 6; 1 cup (250 g) per serving**

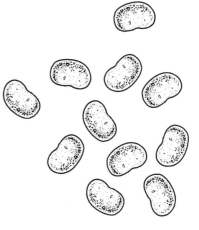

Sausage and Lima Beans with Mustard Sauce

3 fully cooked chicken apple sausage links
  (3 ounces [84 g] each), such as Al Fresco

2 cups (352 g) frozen large Fordhook
  lima beans

1 cup (122 g) frozen sliced carrot

1 cup (235 ml) plus 1½ tablespoons (23 ml)
  water, divided

2 tablespoons (28 g) 2% plain
  Greek yogurt

2 tablespoons (30 g) light mayonnaise

½ teaspoon yellow mustard

Pinch of cayenne pepper

Black pepper to taste

This is such a great "stress-soothing" dish to make when energies are low . . . really low and you're short on time.

1. Diagonally cut the sausage links into ⅛-inch (3 mm)-thick slices.

2. Select Browning/Sauté on the pressure cooker. When the pot is hot, coat it with cooking spray. Add the sausage and cook for 5 minutes or until the edges begin to brown, stirring occasionally. Transfer to a plate and set aside; cover to keep warm.

3. Add the lima beans, carrots, and 1 cup (235 ml) of the water to the pressure cooker pot. Lock the lid in place and close the seal valve. Press the Cancel button, then reset to Manual for 4 minutes.

▶ NUTRITION FACTS

Amount Per Serving

Calories	270	
Calories from Fat	70	
		% Daily Value
Total Fat	8 g	12%
Saturated Fat	2 g	10%
Trans Fat	0 g	
Cholesterol	50 mg	17%
Sodium	460 mg	19%
Total Carbohydrate	32 g	11%
Dietary Fiber	6 g	24%
Sugars	11 g	
Protein	18 g	
Vitamin A		100%
Vitamin C		4%
Calcium		2%
Iron		6%
Magnesium	42 mg	
Potassium	581 mg	

4. Meanwhile, stir together the yogurt, mayonnaise, mustard, cayenne pepper, and remaining 1½ tablespoons (25 ml) water in a small bowl. Set aside.

5. When the cook time ends, use a quick pressure release.

6. When the valve drops, carefully remove the lid. Remove the vegetables with a slotted spoon and divide among 4 bowls. Top with the reserved sausage and the yogurt mixture; sprinkle with the black pepper.

▶ **SERVES 4; About ½ cup (106 g) vegetables, scant ½ cup (50 g) sausage plus 1½ tablespoon sauce per serving**

No-Chop Sausage-Barley Bowls

3 Italian turkey sausage links (3 ounces [84 g] each), casings removed

1/2 cup (100 g) pearl barley, rinsed and drained

2 cups (168 g) frozen peppers and onions

2 cups (248 g) frozen cut green beans

1 cup (122 g) frozen sliced carrots

1 package (8 ounces [225 g]) sliced mushrooms

1 can (14.5 ounces [4106 g]) no-salt-added stewed tomatoes

3/4 cup (175 ml) water

1 tablespoon (15 ml) Worcestershire sauce

2 to 3 teaspoons dried Italian seasoning

2 ounces (55 g) baby spinach

3/4 teaspoon salt

1/2 teaspoon black pepper

1 tablespoon (15 ml) extra virgin olive oil

2 tablespoons (10 g) grated Parmesan cheese

This is one dish where you don't have to pull out your knife . . . leave it in your drawer and savor this hearty dish and the simplicity of it all.

1. Select Browning/Sauté on the pressure cooker. When the pot is hot, coat it with cooking spray. Add the sausages and cook for 4 minutes, breaking up the meat and stirring frequently.

2. Add the barley, peppers and onions, green beans, carrots, mushrooms, tomatoes, water, Worcestershire sauce, and Italian seasoning. Lock the lid in place and close the seal valve. Press the Cancel button and reset to Manual for 20 minutes.

Cook's Note:
If time allows, let the mixture stand for 15 minutes to allow the flavors to blend. This is even better the next day!

Amount Per Serving

Calories	190	
Calories from Fat	60	
		% Daily Value
Total Fat	7 g	11%
Saturated Fat	1 g	5%
Trans Fat	0 g	
Cholesterol	25 mg	8%
Sodium	580 mg	24%
Total Carbohydrate	21 g	7%
Dietary Fiber	5 g	20%
Sugars	6 g	
Protein	11 g	
Vitamin A		80%
Vitamin C		20%
Calcium		8%
Iron		15%
Magnesium	29.58 mg	
Potassium	337.38 mg	

3. When the cook time ends, use a quick pressure release.

4. When the valve drops, carefully remove the lid. Turn off the heat. Stir in the spinach, salt, black pepper, and extra virgin olive oil.

5. Serve topped with the Parmesan cheese.

▸ **SERVES 7; About 1 cup (225 g) per serving**

Smoked Sausage and Spinach Rice

2 tablespoons (28 ml) extra virgin olive oil, divided

8 ounces (225 g) smoked turkey sausage, thinly sliced

1 cup (190 g) brown rice

1½ cups (225 g) chopped red or green bell pepper

1 cup (235 ml) water

½ teaspoon onion powder

¼ teaspoon ground turmeric

4 ounces (115 g) baby spinach

1½ teaspoons smoked paprika

¼ teaspoon black pepper

1 teaspoon hot sauce, such as Frank's

This is a great one to make ahead because the flavors just keep getting better and better.

1. Select Browning/Sauté on the pressure cooker. When the pot is hot, add 1 tablespoon (15 ml) of extra virgin olive oil to the pot. Add the sausage and cook for 4 to 5 minutes or until richly browned on the edges, stirring occasionally. Transfer to a plate and set aside.

2. Add the brown rice, bell pepper, water, onion powder, and turmeric to the pressure cooker pot, scraping up any browned bits. Top with the sausage. Do not stir. Lock the lid in place and close the seal valve. Press the Cancel button and reset to Manual for 20 minutes.

3. When the cook time ends, use a quick pressure release.

4. When the valve drops, carefully remove the lid. Using two utensils, as you would a stir-fry, stir in the spinach, smoked paprika, black pepper, hot sauce, and remaining 1 tablespoon (15 ml) extra virgin olive oil. Stir until spinach has wilted slightly. Cover and let stand for 5 minutes to allow the flavors to blend.

▶ **SERVES 4; 1 cup (225 g) per serving**

▶ **NUTRITION FACTS**

Amount Per Serving

		% Daily Value
Calories	320	
Calories from Fat	90	
Total Fat	10 g	15%
Saturated Fat	2 g	10%
Trans Fat	0 g	
Cholesterol	10 mg	3%
Sodium	520 mg	22%
Total Carbohydrate	47 g	16%
Dietary Fiber	5 g	20%
Sugars	3 g	
Protein	10 g	
Vitamin A		70%
Vitamin C		130%
Calcium		6%
Iron		15%
Magnesium	102.41 mg	
Potassium	324.57 mg	

Beef and Burrito Rice

1 pound (455 g) lean ground beef

1½ cups (240 g) chopped onion

1 can (15 ounces [425 g]) no-salt-added
black beans, rinsed and drained

1½ cups (246 g) frozen corn kernels

1 can (10 ounces [280 g]) tomatoes
with green chiles

1 cup (190 g) brown rice

1 cup (235 ml) water

2 teaspoons smoked paprika

2 teaspoons ground cumin

½ teaspoon ground turmeric

1 teaspoon salt

½ cup (8 g) chopped fresh cilantro
or (50 g) finely chopped green onion

4 ounces (115 g) shredded reduced-fat
sharp cheddar cheese

Kid-friendly comfort . . . enough said!

1. Select Browning/Sauté on the pressure cooker. When the pot is hot, coat it with cooking spray. Add the beef and cook for 4 minutes or until beginning to brown, stirring occasionally.

2. Stir in the onion, black beans, corn, tomatoes, brown rice, water, paprika, cumin, and turmeric. Lock the lid in place and close the seal valve. Press the Manual button for 15 minutes.

3. When the cook time ends, use a natural pressure release.

4. When the valve drops, carefully remove the lid. Stir in the salt and cilantro. Serve topped with equal amounts of cheddar cheese.

▸ **SERVES 8; About 1 cup (210 g) per serving**

▸ **NUTRITION FACTS**

Amount Per Serving

Calories	270	
Calories from Fat	60	
		% Daily Value
Total Fat	7 g	11%
Saturated Fat	3 g	15%
Trans Fat	0 g	
Cholesterol	45 mg	15%
Sodium	580 mg	24%
Total Carbohydrate	33 g	11%
Dietary Fiber	4 g	16%
Sugars	3 g	
Protein	21 g	
Vitamin A		6%
Vitamin C		10%
Calcium		15%
Iron		15%
Magnesium	73.83 mg	
Potassium	418.13 mg	

Cook's Note:
You can also spoon the rice mixture into a 13 x 9-inch (33 x 23 cm) baking dish or 3-quart (2.8 L) casserole, sprinkle evenly with the cheese, and place under the broiler for 1 minute to melt the cheese slightly.

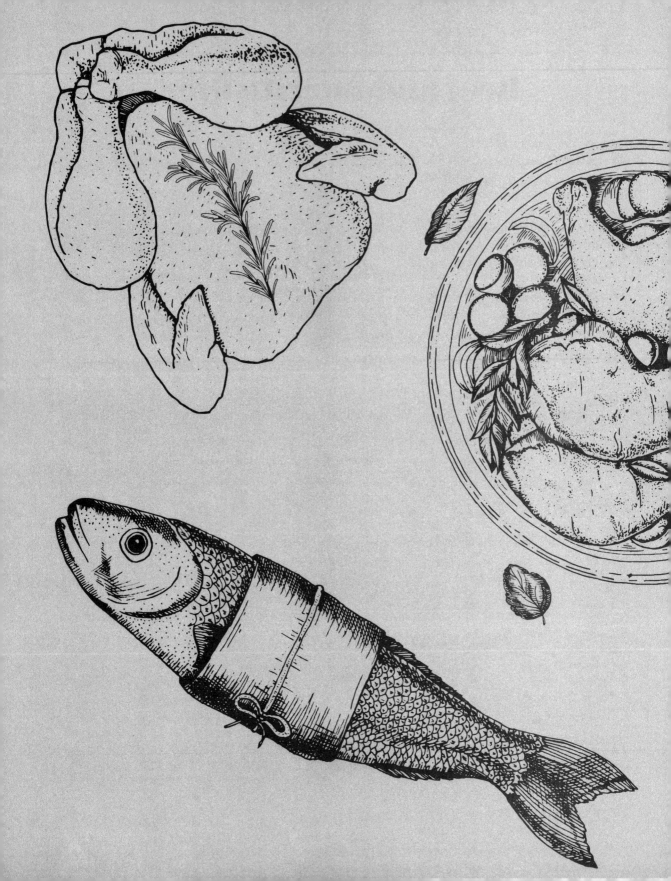

6

Protein and Vegetable Combination Dinners

Italian Cheese and Vegetable Casserole

2 tablespoons (28 ml) extra virgin olive oil, divided

1 large green bell pepper (8 ounces [225 g] total), cored and cut into 1-inch (2.5 cm) pieces

4 ounces (115 g) uncooked whole-grain rotini pasta

12 ounces (340 g) eggplant, cut into 1-inch (2.5 cm) pieces

1 cup (235 ml) white wine

1 tablespoon (15 ml) balsamic vinegar

1 zucchini (7 ounces [200 g] total), halved lengthwise and cut into 1-inch (2.5 cm) slices

1½ cups (270 g) grape tomatoes

1 cup (160 g) chopped onion

1 tablespoon (3 g) dried oregano

½ teaspoon salt

16 kalamata olives, pitted and coarsely chopped

4 ounces (115 g) shredded part-skim mozzarella cheese

1 tablespoon (5 g) grated Parmesan cheese

Here's a nice change from the traditional "pressure cooker dish." Cook it in the pressure cooker and then plop it into a baking dish and run it under the broiler for a minute to give a "casserole" feel. This dish cooks in a fraction of the time while keeping your kitchen cool.

1. Select Browning/Sauté on the pressure cooker. When the pot is hot, add 1 tablespoon (15 ml) of extra virgin olive oil. Tilt the pot to coat the bottom lightly. Add the bell pepper in a single layer and cook for 8 minutes or until beginning to richly brown, stirring occasionally.

2. Add the pasta, eggplant, white wine, and balsamic vinegar, making sure the pasta is immersed in the liquid. Top with the zucchini, tomatoes, onion, and oregano. Do not stir. Lock the lid in place and close the seal valve. Press the Cancel button and reset to Manual for 4 minutes.

▸ **NUTRITION FACTS**

Amount Per Serving

Calories	270	
Calories from Fat	110	

		% Daily Value
Total Fat	13 g	20%
Saturated Fat	3.5 g	18%
Trans Fat	0 g	
Cholesterol	10 mg	3%
Sodium	530 mg	22%
Total Carbohydrate	26 g	9%
Dietary Fiber	5 g	20%
Sugars	7 g	
Protein	10 g	

Vitamin A	15%
Vitamin C	70%
Calcium	20%
Iron	8%
Magnesium	28.68 mg
Potassium	440.39 mg

3. When the cook time ends, use a quick pressure release.

4. When the valve drops, carefully remove the lid. Remove the vegetables and pasta with a slotted spoon and place in an 11 x 7-inch (28 x 18 cm) or 2-quart (1.8 L) broiler safe casserole dish. Sprinkle evenly with the salt and kalamata olives. Top with the cheeses and place under the broiler for 1 to 2 minutes or until the cheese has melted and is just beginning to turn golden, watching carefully not to burn.

▸ **SERVES 6; About 1¼ cups (244 g) per serving**

Lemon-Dill Fish with Potatoes and Green Beans

1/4 cup (55 g) light butter with canola oil

1 teaspoon dried dill

1/4 teaspoon paprika, plus more for sprinkling

Grated zest from 1 lemon

3/4 teaspoon salt

1/4 teaspoon black pepper

2 cups (475 ml) water

1 pound (455 g) petite potatoes, quartered (about 1 inch [2.5 cm] in diameter)

12 ounces (340 g) green beans, stemmed

2 large lettuce leaves, such as romaine

4 cod fillets (4-ounce [112 g] each)

1 lemon, cut into 4 wedges, optional

Whole lettuce leaves are used to separate the delicate pieces of fish from the other chunkier ingredients.

1. Combine the butter, dill, paprika, lemon zest, salt, and pepper in a small bowl. Stir until well blended. Set aside.

2. Place the water and steamer basket in the pressure cooker pot and top with the potatoes and green beans. Place the lettuce leaves over the vegetables; top with the cod fillets and sprinkle with paprika. Lock the lid in place and close the seal valve. Press the Manual button for 3 minutes.

▸ NUTRITION FACTS

Amount Per Serving

Calories	240	
Calories from Fat	50	
		% Daily Value
Total Fat	6 g	9%
Saturated Fat	2 g	10%
Trans Fat	0 g	
Cholesterol	55 mg	18%
Sodium	460 mg	19%
Total Carbohydrate	23 g	8%
Dietary Fiber	5 g	20%
Sugars	4 g	
Protein	23 g	
Vitamin A		15%
Vitamin C		30%
Calcium		8%
Iron		10%
Magnesium	61.24 mg	
Potassium	1189.29 mg	

3. When the cook time ends, use a quick pressure release.

4. When the valve drops, carefully remove the lid. Check the cod fillets for doneness. Remove the fillets and place on 4 individual dinner plates. Discard the lettuce leaves. Remove the vegetables and steamer basket. Discard the water. Return the vegetables to the pot with the butter mixture and toss gently until well coated. Spoon equal amounts over each serving of fish. Serve with lemon wedges, if desired.

▸ **SERVES 4; 3 ounces (85 g) fish plus 1½ cups (199 g) vegetables per serving**

Ginger-Peach Salmon

TOPPING:

2 cups (475 ml) water

8 ounces (225 g) frozen sliced peaches

1/8 teaspoon crushed red pepper flakes, optional

1 1/2 tablespoons (20 g) sugar

1 teaspoon grated ginger

1 teaspoon balsamic vinegar

1/4 teaspoon vanilla extract

FISH:

4 salmon fillets (4-ounce [115 g] each)

Paprika

1/2 teaspoon ground cumin

1/4 teaspoon salt

1 red bell pepper, cored and cut into thin strips

Adding a small amount of vanilla to the peaches provides a subtle flavor while helping to tie the ingredients together.

1. To make the topping: Place the water and a steamer basket in the pressure cooker pot. Top with the peaches and sprinkle with the red pepper flakes. Lock the lid in place and close the seal valve. Press the Manual button for 1 minute.

2. When the cook time ends, use a quick pressure release.

3. When the valve drops, carefully remove the lid. Place the peaches in a medium bowl and add the sugar, ginger, balsamic vinegar, and vanilla. Stir gently and set aside.

4. To make the fish: Place the salmon in the steamer basket and sprinkle with the paprika, cumin, and salt, then place the bell pepper on top. Press the Cancel button and reset to Manual for 2 minutes.

Cook's Note:

For fillets that are 1 inch (2.5 cm) thick or thicker, cook the fillets for 3 minutes.

▸ NUTRITION FACTS

Amount Per Serving

Calories	210
Calories from Fat	70

		% Daily Value
Total Fat	7 g	11%
Saturated Fat	1 g	5%
Trans Fat	0 g	
Cholesterol	60 mg	20%
Sodium	200 mg	8%
Total Carbohydrate	12 g	4%
Dietary Fiber	1 g	4%
Sugars	11 g	
Protein	23 g	

Vitamin A		25%
Vitamin C		150%
Calcium		2%
Iron		6%
Magnesium	36.71 mg	
Potassium	693.91 mg	

5. When the cook time ends, use a quick pressure release.

6. When the valve drops, carefully remove the lid. Check the salmon for doneness. Transfer the fillets to 4 dinner plates and top with equal amounts of the peach mixture.

▸ **SERVES 4; 3 ounces (85 g) fish, 1 ounce (28 g) bell pepper and 3 tablespoons (45 g) peach mixture per serving**

Lime Salmon and Maple Butternut Squash

3 tablespoons (45 ml) pure maple syrup

2 teaspoons sriracha sauce

½ teaspoon salt, divided

1 cup (235 ml) water

4 salmon fillets (4 ounces [115 g] each)

¼ teaspoon dried thyme leaves

1 pound (455 g) peeled and chopped butternut squash

1 lime, halved

¼ teaspoon black pepper

Sometimes, the simplest sauces are the sensational sauces. By simply mixing maple syrup with hot sauce, you have a sweet heat that ties this dish together. And a splash of fresh lime over the salmon brightens the whole dish.

1. Whisk together the maple syrup, sriracha, and ⅛ teaspoon of the salt in a small bowl and set aside.

2. Place the water and a steamer basket in the pressure cooker pot. Place the salmon in the basket and sprinkle with the thyme. Surround the salmon with the squash and sprinkle with ¼ teaspoon of the salt. Lock the lid in place and close the seal valve. Press the Manual button for 3 minutes.

Amount Per Serving

Calories	250
Calories from Fat	60

		% Daily Value
Total Fat	6 g	9%
Saturated Fat	1 g	5%
Trans Fat	0 g	
Cholesterol	60 mg	20%
Sodium	410 mg	17%
Total Carbohydrate	24 g	8%
Dietary Fiber	2 g	8%
Sugars	12 g	
Protein	25 g	

Vitamin A	240%
Vitamin C	45%
Calcium	8%
Iron	8%
Magnesium	42.33 mg
Potassium	440.03 mg

3. When the cook time ends, use a quick pressure release.

4. When the valve drops, carefully remove the lid. Check the salmon for doneness. Squeeze lime juice evenly over the salmon. Serve the squash alongside the salmon and sprinkle all with the remaining ⅛ teaspoon salt and the pepper. Drizzle the maple syrup mixture evenly over the squash.

▸ **SERVES 4; 3 ounces (85 g) salmon, about ¾ cup (90 g) squash, plus about 1 tablespoon (15 ml) sauce per serving**

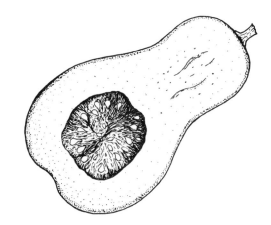

Sweet Thai Salmon on Asparagus

1 cup (235 ml) water

1 pound (455 g) asparagus spears, ends trimmed

¼ teaspoon salt

1 pound (455 g) fresh or frozen salmon fillets

¼ teaspoon pepper

2 lemons, divided

¼ cup (56 g) sweet chili sauce, Thai variety

1 avocado, peeled, pitted, and chopped

¼ cup (24 g) chopped fresh mint or (4 g) cilantro

Overcooking fish can serve up dry results. That's why it's very important to pay attention to the thickness of the fish fillets. A general rule is if it's thinner than 1 inch (2.5 cm), cook for 3 minutes. If it's thicker than 1 inch (2.5 cm), cook it for 4—never more!

1. Place the water and a steamer basket in the pressure cooker pot. Arrange the asparagus on top. Lock the lid in place and close the seal valve. Press the Manual button for 1 minute.

2. When the cook time ends, use a quick pressure release.

3. When the valve drops, carefully remove the lid. Remove the asparagus, sprinkle with the salt, and set aside.

4. Place the salmon in the steamer basket. Sprinkle with the pepper. Lock the lid in place and close the seal valve. Press the Cancel button and reset to Manual for 3 minutes.

▸ NUTRITION FACTS

Amount Per Serving

Calories	280	
Calories from Fat	110	
		% Daily Value
Total Fat	12 g	18%
Saturated Fat	2 g	10%
Trans Fat	0 g	
Cholesterol	60 mg	20%
Sodium	400 mg	17%
Total Carbohydrate	17 g	6%
Dietary Fiber	5 g	20%
Sugars	10 g	
Protein	26 g	
Vitamin A		15%
Vitamin C		30%
Calcium		4%
Iron		8%
Magnesium	43.47 mg	
Potassium	1021.57 mg	

5. When the cook time ends, use a quick pressure release.

6. When the valve drops, carefully remove the lid. Check the salmon for doneness. Remove the salmon, roughly flake, and place on top of the asparagus. Squeeze the juice of 1 lemon evenly over all and spoon the chili sauce on top. Sprinkle with the avocado and mint. Serve with the remaining lemon cut into 4 wedges.

▸ **SERVES 4; 3 ounces (85 g) salmon, about 3½ ounces (99 g) cooked asparagus, ¼ avocado (50 g), and 1 tablespoon (15 ml) sauce per serving**

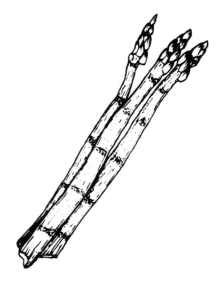

Turmeric-Ginger Chicken with Carrots

1 tablespoon (15 ml) canola oil

12 ounces (340 g) boneless, skinless chicken thighs, cut into 1½-inch (3.8 cm) chunks

2 cups (244 g) frozen sliced carrots

1 can (8 ounces [225 g]) no-salt-added tomato sauce

½ cup (120 ml) water

2 teaspoons ground cumin, divided

½ teaspoon ground turmeric

½ cup (8 g) chopped fresh cilantro

2 tablespoons (28 g) light butter with canola oil

1 tablespoon (8 g) grated ginger

2 teaspoons sugar

1 teaspoon curry powder

½ teaspoon salt

1 pouch (8.5 ounces [238 g]) basmati rice, such as Ready Rice

Adding a portion of ground cumin at the end will make the taste of the cumin more pronounced without leaving the dish overly pungent.

1. Select Browning/Sauté on the pressure cooker. When the pot is hot, add the canola oil. Tilt the pot to lightly coat the bottom. Add the chicken in a single layer and cook for 4 minutes on one side. Do NOT stir. (Note: It may build up residue on the bottom, but that will add to the flavor of the dish.)

2. Stir in the carrots, tomato sauce, water, 1 teaspoon of the cumin, and turmeric. Lock the lid in place and close the seal valve. Press the Cancel button and reset to Manual for 5 minutes.

▸ NUTRITION FACTS

Amount Per Serving

Calories	310	
Calories from Fat	100	

		% Daily Value
Total Fat	12 g	18%
Saturated Fat	3 g	15%
Trans Fat	0 g	
Cholesterol	85 mg	28%
Sodium	480 mg	20%
Total Carbohydrate	32 g	11%
Dietary Fiber	4 g	16%
Sugars	8 g	
Protein	21 g	

Vitamin A		200%
Vitamin C		15%
Calcium		4%
Iron		10%
Magnesium	28.41 mg	
Potassium	372.96 mg	

3. When the cook time ends, use a natural pressure release.

4. When the valve drops, carefully remove the lid. Check the chicken for doneness. Stir in the remaining 1 teaspoon cumin, cilantro, butter, ginger, sugar, curry powder, and salt.

5. Cook the rice according to the package directions.

6. Divide the rice among 4 bowls and top with the chicken and carrots.

▸ **SERVES 4; 1 cup (225 g) chicken mixture plus about ½ cup (about 90 g) rice per serving**

Provençal Chicken and New Potatoes

4 bone-in chicken thighs (about 2 pounds [900 g] total), skin removed

1 cup (235 ml) dry white wine

8 cloves garlic, peeled

1 teaspoon poultry seasoning

¼ teaspoon dried rosemary

½ teaspoon onion powder

¼ teaspoon black pepper

¼ teaspoon paprika

2 pounds (900 g) petite potatoes, about 1 inch (2.5 cm) in diameter

1 tablespoon (15 ml) water

1 tablespoon (8 g) cornstarch

¾ teaspoon salt

¼ cup (25 g) finely chopped green onion

This comforting, bistro-style dish is made all in one pot. Make sure the potassium-loaded potatoes are about the same size, or they will not cook evenly.

1. Place the chicken and white wine in the pressure cooker pot. Sprinkle with the garlic, poultry seasoning, rosemary, onion powder, pepper, and paprika and top with the potatoes. Lock the lid in place and close the seal valve. Press the Manual button for 15 minutes.

2. When the cook time ends, use a quick pressure release.

3. When the valve drops, carefully remove the lid. Check the chicken for doneness. Transfer the potatoes and chicken to a bowl using a slotted spoon.

Cook's Note:
If the potatoes are larger than 1 inch (2.5 cm), cut them in half.

Amount Per Serving

Calories	430	
Calories from Fat	90	

		% Daily Value
Total Fat	10 g	15%
Saturated Fat	3 g	15%
Trans Fat	0 g	
Cholesterol	90 mg	30%
Sodium	560 mg	23%
Total Carbohydrate	42 g	14%
Dietary Fiber	4 g	16%
Sugars	4 g	
Protein	30 g	

Vitamin A		2%
Vitamin C		40%
Calcium		6%
Iron		20%
Magnesium	78.85 mg	
Potassium	1302.73 mg	

4. Reset to Browning/Sauté. Whisk together the water and cornstarch in a small bowl and then stir into the pan drippings along with the salt. Bring to a boil and boil 1 to 1½ minutes or until thickened slightly, breaking up the garlic with a whisk.

5. Pour the sauce over the chicken and potatoes and sprinkle with the green onion.

▸ **SERVES 4; 1½ cups (230 g) potatoes, 3 ounces (85 g) chicken, and ⅓ cup (80 ml) sauce per serving**

Bayou Chicken Thighs on Crookneck Squash

12 ounces (340 g) yellow crookneck squash, very thinly sliced

½ cup (75 g) chopped green bell pepper

¼ teaspoon black pepper

¼ teaspoon plus ⅛ teaspoon salt, divided

½ cup (120 ml) water

4 boneless, skinless chicken thighs (4 ounces [115 g]), trimmed of fat

1 can (8 ounces [225 g]) no-salt-added tomato sauce

1 teaspoon dried thyme

½ teaspoon garlic powder

1 tablespoon (15 ml) hot sauce, such as Frank's

2 teaspoons Worcestershire sauce

¼ cup (15 g) chopped fresh parsley

We get in the habit of thinking that there needs to be a rice, potato, or pasta base to our dishes. Serve saucy dishes over veggies instead: it brings new interest to the table and gets you away from some of those carbs.

1. Select Browning/Sauté on the pressure cooker. When the pot is hot, coat it with cooking spray. Add the yellow squash, bell pepper, and black pepper. Cook for 5 minutes, or until the squash is just tender crisp stirring frequently. Transfer to a plate, sprinkle with ⅛ teaspoon of the salt, and cover to keep warm.

2. Add the water to the pressure cooker pot and scrape the bottom to release any browned bits. Add the chicken, tomato sauce, thyme, garlic powder, hot sauce, and Worcestershire sauce. Lock the lid in place and close the seal valve. Press the Cancel button, then reset to Manual for 8 minutes.

▶ NUTRITION FACTS

Amount Per Serving

Calories	200
Calories from Fat	80

		% Daily Value
Total Fat	9 g	14%
Saturated Fat	2.5 g	13%
Trans Fat	0 g	
Cholesterol	75 mg	25%
Sodium	450 mg	19%
Total Carbohydrate	8 g	3%
Dietary Fiber	2 g	8%
Sugars	5 g	
Protein	23 g	

Vitamin A		20%
Vitamin C		70%
Calcium		4%
Iron		15%
Magnesium	47.25 mg	
Potassium	593.67 mg	

3. When the cook time ends, use a quick pressure release.

4. When the valve drops, carefully remove the lid. Check the chicken for doneness. Using a slotted spoon, place the chicken on top of the squash; cover to keep warm.

5. Press the Cancel button and reset to Browning/Sauté. Add the remaining 1/4 teaspoon salt and bring the sauce to a boil. Cook for 5 minutes, or until the liquid is reduced to 1 cup (235 ml). Spoon over all and sprinkle with the parsley.

▶ **SERVES 4; 3/4 cup (135 g) squash, 3 ounces (85 g) chicken and 1/4 cup (60 g) sauce per serving**

Chicken with Mushrooms, Brandy, and Bacon

3 ounces (85 g) sliced bacon

8 ounces (225 g) sliced mushrooms

4 bone-in chicken thighs (about 2 pounds [900 g] total), skin removed

9 ounces (255 g) carrots, cut into 4-inch (10 cm) pieces

1/2 cup (120 ml) water

1/2 cup (120 ml) brandy (or Marsala)

1 tablespoon (16 g) tomato paste

1 teaspoon paprika

1/2 teaspoon dried thyme

1 dried bay leaf

1/2 teaspoon garlic powder

1/4 teaspoon black pepper

1/4 cup (25 g) chopped green onion

1/2 teaspoon salt

No brandy in the house? You don't have to buy a large bottle, as very small bottles are available. And if you're not a brandy lover, you can use Marsala, Madeira, or even sherry. The choice is yours.

1. Press Browning/Sauté on the pressure cooker. When the pot is hot, add the bacon and cook for 5 minutes or until crisp. Set the bacon aside on paper towels to drain. Discard all but 1 tablespoon (15 ml) of the bacon drippings.

2. Add the mushrooms to the 1 tablespoon (15 ml) bacon drippings and cook for 5 minutes or until beginning to lightly brown, stirring occasionally. Add the chicken, carrots, and water.

3. Whisk together the brandy and tomato paste in a small bowl. Pour evenly over all and sprinkle with the paprika, thyme, bay leaf, garlic powder, and pepper. Lock the lid in place and close the seal valve. Press the Cancel button and reset to Manual for 18 minutes.

▸ NUTRITION FACTS

Amount Per Serving

Calories	340	
Calories from Fat	110	

		% Daily Value
Total Fat	12 g	18%
Saturated Fat	4 g	20%
Trans Fat	0 g	
Cholesterol	140 mg	47%
Sodium	600 mg	25%
Total Carbohydrate	9 g	3%
Dietary Fiber	3 g	12%
Sugars	4 g	
Protein	32 g	

Vitamin A		210%
Vitamin C		10%
Calcium		4%
Iron		10%
Magnesium	46.48 mg	
Potassium	774.02 mg	

4. When the cook time ends, use a 10-minute natural pressure release, then a quick pressure release.

5. When the valve drops, carefully remove the lid. Check the chicken for doneness. Remove the chicken and carrots with a slotted spoon and place in a rimmed bowl or baking pan.

6. Stir the reserved bacon, green onion, and salt into the mushrooms in the pressure cooker pot. Press the Cancel button and reset to Browning/Sauté. Bring to a boil and cook for 5 minutes or until reduced to 2 cups (475 ml). Remove the bay leaf. Pour the mushroom and bacon sauce over the chicken and carrots.

▸ **SERVES 4; 1 chicken thigh (85 g), about 2 ounces (55 g) carrots, and ½ cup (106 g) mushroom mixture per serving**

Beer-Braised Chicken with Poblano Chiles and Cheese

2 boneless, skinless chicken breasts
(8 ounces [227 g] each)

1 cup (235 ml) light beer, such as
Miller Lite

1 teaspoon smoked paprika

½ teaspoon ground cumin

½ teaspoon garlic powder

2 medium poblano peppers, chopped

¼ cup (60 ml) fat-free milk

2 teaspoons cornstarch

½ teaspoon Worcestershire sauce

¼ teaspoon salt

2 ounces (55 g) shredded reduced-fat
sharp cheddar cheese

The heat from the sauce helps melt the cheese ever so slightly. Serve with broccoli florets for an invitingly colorful dish.

1. Place the chicken and beer in the pressure cooker pot, sprinkle with the smoked paprika, cumin, and garlic powder, and top with the poblano peppers. Lock the lid in place and close the seal valve. Press the Manual button for 6 minutes.

2. When the cook time ends, use a 5-minute natural pressure release, then a quick pressure release.

3. When the valve drops, carefully remove the lid. Check the chicken doneness. Remove the chicken with a slotted spoon and let stand on a cutting board for 5 minutes before slicing.

4. Meanwhile, place a colander over a bowl. Drain the pepper mixture in the colander. Return the drained peppers and ½ cup (120 ml) of the liquid to the pot, discarding any remaining liquid.

Amount Per Serving		
Calories	220	
Calories from Fat	60	
		% Daily Value
Total Fat	6 g	9%
Saturated Fat	2.5 g	13%
Trans Fat	0 g	
Cholesterol	95 mg	32%
Sodium	300 mg	13%
Total Carbohydrate	8 g	3%
Dietary Fiber	1 g	4%
Sugars	3 g	
Protein	31 g	
Vitamin A		15%
Vitamin C		170%
Calcium		15%
Iron		6%
Magnesium	48.02 mg	
Potassium	559.39 mg	

5. Whisk together the milk and cornstarch in a small bowl, stirring until the cornstarch is dissolved. Stir into the poblano pepper mixture in the pot and add the Worcestershire sauce and salt.

6. Press the Cancel button and reset to Browning/Sauté. Bring the pepper mixture to a boil and cook for 3 minutes, or until slightly thickened.

7. Place equal amounts of the chicken on each of 4 dinner plates, top with the pepper mixture, and sprinkle with the cheese.

► **SERVES 4; 3 ounces (85 g) chicken, ¼ cup (60 g) pepper sauce, and ½ ounce (15 g) cheese per serving**

Ginger-Lime Chicken and Broccoli Bowls

4 bone-in chicken thighs (about
  13/4 pounds [795 g] total), skin removed

1/2 teaspoon black pepper

1/2 teaspoon paprika

1 cup (235 ml) water

1 teaspoon grated ginger

2 tablespoons (28 ml) lime juice

2 tablespoons (28 ml) apple cider vinegar

3 tablespoons (45 ml) reduced-sodium
  soy sauce

3 tablespoons (60 g) honey

1/8 teaspoon crushed red pepper flakes,
  optional

12 ounces (340 g) broccoli florets

This is like a reverse marinade: the assertive ingredients are added at the end and the cooked chicken soaks up the flavors while it rests.

1. Sprinkle the smooth side of the chicken with the pepper and paprika. Pour the water into the pressure cooker pot and top with the chicken, overlapping slightly if necessary. Lock the lid in place and close the seal valve. Press the Manual button for 20 minutes.

2. When the cook time ends, use a natural pressure release for 10 minutes, then a quick pressure release.

3. When the valve drops, carefully remove the lid. Check the chicken for doneness. Remove the chicken with a slotted spoon and place, smooth-side up, in each of 4 shallow soup bowls.

Amount Per Serving		
Calories	230	
Calories from Fat	45	
		% Daily Value
Total Fat	5 g	8%
Saturated Fat	1.5 g	8%
Trans Fat	0 g	
Cholesterol	110 mg	37%
Sodium	460 mg	19%
Total Carbohydrate	20 g	7%
Dietary Fiber	3 g	12%
Sugars	13 g	
Protein	27 g	
Vitamin A		50%
Vitamin C		140%
Calcium		6%
Iron		10%
Magnesium	53.62 mg	
Potassium	932.04 mg	

4. In a small bowl, whisk together the ginger, lime juice, apple cider vinegar, soy sauce, honey, and red pepper flakes (if using) and spoon evenly over the chicken. Cover and let stand for 10 minutes to allow the flavors to blend.

5. Meanwhile, press the Cancel button. Select Browning/ Sauté. Bring the liquid in the pot to a boil, add the broccoli, return to a boil, cover (do not lock lid), and cook for 3 minutes, or until tender crisp. Remove the broccoli with a slotted spoon and arrange around the chicken and sauce.

▶ **SERVES 4; 4 ounces (115 g) chicken, 2 tablespoons (28 ml) sauce, and 1 cup (71 g) broccoli per serving**

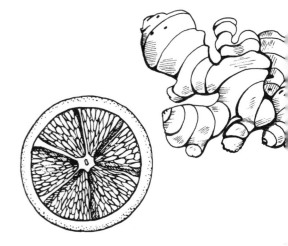

Chicken and Okra Creole Style

4 bone-in chicken thighs (about 2 pounds [900 g]), skin removed

2 cups (300 g) chopped green bell pepper

1 cup (160 g) chopped onion

3 cups (360 g) fresh or frozen cut okra

1 can (14.5 ounces [410 g]) no-salt-added stewed tomatoes

1/2 cup (120 ml) water

2 dried bay leaves

1 teaspoon dried thyme

1/2 teaspoon garlic powder

1/4 teaspoon cayenne pepper

2 tablespoons (30 g) ketchup

1 tablespoon (15 ml) apple cider vinegar

1/4 cup (15 g) chopped fresh parsley

1 teaspoon salt

This dish is a Deep South favorite. Top with a bit of rice and a splash of hot sauce for even more of that Bayou taste. An 8-ounce (225 g) package of prepared whole-grain rice is a perfect amount, with about 1/3 cup (47 g) cooked rice per serving.

1. Combine the chicken, bell pepper, onion, okra, tomatoes, water, bay leaves, thyme, garlic powder, and cayenne pepper in the pressure cooker pot.

2. In a small bowl, stir together the ketchup and apple cider vinegar; spoon evenly over all. Do NOT stir. Lock the lid in place and close the seal valve. Press the Manual button for 15 minutes.

Amount Per Serving

Calories	180	
Calories from Fat	35	
		% Daily Value
Total Fat	4 g	6%
Saturated Fat	1 g	5%
Trans Fat	0 g	
Cholesterol	85 mg	28%
Sodium	550 mg	23%
Total Carbohydrate	14 g	5%
Dietary Fiber	4 g	16%
Sugars	8 g	
Protein	20 g	
Vitamin A		10%
Vitamin C		80%
Calcium		8%
Iron		10%
Magnesium	29.25 mg	
Potassium	444.94 mg	

3. When the cook time ends, use a quick pressure release.

4. When the valve drops, carefully remove the lid. Check the chicken for doneness. Remove the chicken with slotted spoon and place on a cutting board. Let stand for 5 minutes before roughly shredding. Return the chicken to the okra mixture and stir in the parsley and salt. Remove the bay leaves. Serve in 6 shallow soup bowls.

▸ **SERVES 6; about 1¹/3 cups (284 g) per serving**

Cumin Turkey and Corn–Stuffed Peppers

4 large multicolored bell peppers

12 ounces (340 g) 93% lean ground turkey

1/2 cup (82 g) frozen corn, thawed

3/8 cup (160 g) plus 1/4 cup (64 g) picante sauce, divided

1/2 cup (8 g) chopped fresh cilantro, divided

1 egg

2 teaspoons ground cumin

1 cup (235 ml) water

2 ounces (55 g) shredded reduced-fat sharp cheddar cheese

When purchasing bell peppers, choose the brightest of colors, such as red, orange, and yellow, to add color and vitamin C.

1. Cut off the top portion of each bell pepper and chop the top portion only. Discard the core and seeds.

2. Combine the ground turkey, chopped bell pepper, corn, 3/8 cup (160 g) of the picante sauce, 1/4 cup (4 g) of the cilantro, egg, and cumin in a medium bowl. Stuff the peppers with the turkey mixture.

3. Place the water and a trivet in the pressure cooker pot and arrange the stuffed peppers on the trivet. Top each pepper with 1 tablespoon (16 g) picante sauce. Lock the lid in place and close the seal valve. Press the Manual button for 15 minutes.

Cook's Note:
Thaw frozen vegetables quickly by placing in a colander and running under cold water briefly until they are pliable. Be sure to drain well before continuing with your recipe.

▶ NUTRITION FACTS

Amount Per Serving

Calories	270	
Calories from Fat	110	
		% Daily Value
Total Fat	12 g	18%
Saturated Fat	4 g	20%
Trans Fat	0 g	
Cholesterol	120 mg	40%
Sodium	510 mg	21%
Total Carbohydrate	18 g	6%
Dietary Fiber	4 g	16%
Sugars	8 g	
Protein	24 g	
Vitamin A		70%
Vitamin C		460%
Calcium		15%
Iron		10%
Magnesium	47.77 mg	
Potassium	624.14 mg	

4. When the cook time ends, use a natural pressure release.

5. When the valve drops, carefully remove the lid. Check the ground turkey mixture for doneness. Remove the stuffed peppers and top with equal amounts of the cheddar cheese and the remaining ¼ cup (4 g) cilantro.

▶ **SERVES 4; 1 stuffed pepper (281 g) per serving**

Down-Home Turkey Meatloaf and Acorn Squash

1 cup (235 ml) water

1/3 cup (82 g) no-salt-added tomato sauce

3 tablespoons (45 g) ketchup

2 teaspoons Worcestershire sauce

12 ounces (340 g) 93% lean ground turkey

1 cup (150 g) chopped green bell pepper

2/3 cup (53 g) quick-cooking oats

1 egg

1 teaspoon dried thyme

1/4 teaspoon plus 1/8 teaspoon salt, divided

1½ pounds (680 g) acorn squash, quartered and seeded

4 teaspoons light butter with canola oil

4 teaspoons packed dark brown sugar

No heating the oven, no boiling big pots of water—it's all done in one pot and the kitchen stays cool.

1. Place a trivet in the pressure cooker pot and add the water.

2. Combine the tomato sauce, ketchup, and Worcestershire sauce in a small bowl.

3. Combine the ground turkey, bell pepper, oats, egg, thyme, 1/4 teaspoon of the salt, and 3 tablespoons (46 g) of the tomato sauce mixture in a medium bowl. On a dinner plate, shape into a loaf about 4 x 6 x 1½ inches (10 x 15 x 4 cm).

4. Cut three sheets of aluminum foil to 18 inches (45 cm). Fold each of the foil sheets in half lengthwise and coat the foil strips with cooking spray. Crisscross the strips in a spoke-like fashion to act as a sling. Place the meatloaf in the center of the spokes. Lift the ends of the foil strips to transfer the loaf to the trivet. Fold down the ends of the foil strips so they won't interfere with closing the lid. Lock the lid in place and close the seal valve. Press the Manual button for 35 minutes.

Amount Per Serving

Calories	310	
Calories from Fat	100	

		% Daily Value
Total Fat	11 g	17%
Saturated Fat	3 g	15%
Trans Fat	0 g	
Cholesterol	110 mg	37%
Sodium	480 mg	20%
Total Carbohydrate	35 g	12%
Dietary Fiber	4 g	16%
Sugars	12 g	
Protein	21 g	

Vitamin A		20%
Vitamin C		80%
Calcium		10%
Iron		20%
Magnesium	69.96 mg	
Potassium	837.47 mg	

5. When the cook time ends, use a quick pressure release.

6. When the valve drops, carefully remove the lid. Check the meatloaf for doneness. Remove the meatloaf carefully using the ends of the foil and place the foil and meatloaf on a cutting board. Spoon the remaining tomato sauce mixture evenly over the meatloaf and let stand for 10 minutes before slicing.

7. Meanwhile, place the acorn squash on the trivet, lock the lid in place, and close the seal valve. Press the Cancel button and reset to Manual for 5 minutes.

8. When the cook time ends, use a 10-minute natural release.

9. When the valve drops, carefully remove the lid. Top each squash quarter with 1 teaspoon of light butter and 1 teaspoon of brown sugar and sprinkle with the remaining 1/8 teaspoon of salt. Serve alongside the meatloaf.

▶ **SERVES 4; ¼ meatloaf (170 g) and 1 squash wedge (149 g) per serving**

Sausage and Cheese–Stuffed Potatoes

2 Italian turkey sausage links (3 ounces [85 g] each), casings removed

½ teaspoon smoked paprika

2 cups (475 ml) water

4 russet potatoes (8 ounces [225 g] each), pierced in several areas with a fork

1 ounce (28 g) shredded reduced-fat sharp cheddar cheese

1 ounce (28 g) crumbled reduced-fat blue cheese

½ cup (50 g) finely chopped green onion (green and white parts)

⅛ teaspoon salt

¼ teaspoon black pepper

Sometimes, potatoes can be dry unless you add tons of butter. But there won't be that kind of problem using this technique . . . and you definitely won't miss the butter.

1. Select Browning/Sauté on the pressure cooker. When the pot is hot, coat it with cooking spray. Add the sausage and paprika and cook for 4 minutes, stirring frequently. Transfer to a medium bowl and set aside.

2. Put a trivet in the pressure cooker pot and add the water. Top with the potatoes. Lock the lid in place and close the seal valve. Press the Cancel button and reset to Manual for 18 minutes.

3. Meanwhile, add the cheddar cheese, blue cheese, and green onion to the sausage in the bowl; toss gently to combine and set aside.

4. When the cook time ends, use a natural pressure release.

5. When the valve drops, carefully remove the lid. Remove the potatoes with tongs (or a fork).

6. Turn on the broiler. Split each potato *almost* in half and place on a baking sheet. Using a fork, fluff the potatoes, being sure to fluff down to the bottom without tearing the potato skin. Sprinkle the salt and pepper evenly over all. Spoon equal amounts of the sausage mixture on top of each potato, covering the surface of the potato, and broil for 2 minutes, or until the cheese has melted slightly.

▶ **SERVES 4; 1 potato (227 g) and ½ cup (51 g) topping per serving**

▶ NUTRITION FACTS

Amount Per Serving

Calories	300	
Calories from Fat	70	
		% Daily Value
Total Fat	7 g	11%
Saturated Fat	3.5 g	18%
Trans Fat	0 g	
Cholesterol	35 mg	12%
Sodium	500 mg	21%
Total Carbohydrate	43 g	14%
Dietary Fiber	4 g	16%
Sugars	2 g	
Protein	16 g	
Vitamin A		4%
Vitamin C		25%
Calcium		15%
Iron		15%
Magnesium	54.08 mg	
Potassium	985.22 mg	

Fresh Collards with Sausage

10 ounces (280 g) smoked turkey sausage, cut into 1/4-inch (6 mm)-thick slices

1 package (16 ounces [455 g]) chopped fresh collard greens

1 cup (235 ml) water

1 tablespoon (15 ml) extra virgin olive oil

2 teaspoons sugar

1/2 teaspoon garlic powder

1/8 teaspoon crushed red pepper flakes

The secret's in the sugar! A small amount will cut the bitterness of the collards, adding mellowness, not sweetness. This is delicious served with grits, too.

1. Press Browning/Sauté on the pressure cooker. When the pot is hot, coat it with cooking spray. Add the sausage and cook for 5 minutes or until richly browned on the edges, stirring occasionally.

2. Add the collards, water, extra virgin olive oil, sugar, garlic powder, and red pepper flakes to the pressure cooker pot. Lock the lid in place and close the seal valve. Press the Cancel button and reset to Manual for 20 minutes.

3. When the cook time ends, use a quick pressure release.

4. When the valve drops, carefully remove the lid. Divide among 4 shallow soup bowls.

▸ **SERVES 4; 1¼ cups (227 g) per serving**

▸ **NUTRITION FACTS**

Amount Per Serving		
Calories	150	
Calories from Fat	50	
		% Daily Value
Total Fat	6 g	9%
Saturated Fat	1 g	5%
Trans Fat	0 g	
Cholesterol	15 mg	5%
Sodium	580 mg	24%
Total Carbohydrate	16 g	5%
Dietary Fiber	5 g	20%
Sugars	3 g	
Protein	9 g	
Vitamin A		110%
Vitamin C		70%
Calcium		25%
Iron		10%
Magnesium	41.96 mg	
Potassium	413.80mg	

Pork Roast, Sweet Potatoes, and Sweet-Spiced Mustard

PORK ROAST:

1 tablespoon (15 ml) canola oil

2 pounds (900 g) trimmed boneless pork shoulder, cut into 4 pieces

2 cups (475 ml) water

1 large onion, cut into 8 wedges (about 6 ounces [170 g] total)

1½ teaspoons dried sage

1 teaspoon paprika

1 teaspoon garlic powder

1 teaspoon black pepper

2 pounds (900 g) sweet potatoes, peeled and cut into 1-inch (2.5 cm) chunks

½ teaspoon salt

SAUCE:

¼ cup (60 g) Dijon mustard

¼ cup (50 g) sugar

2 tablespoons (28 ml) water

⅛ teaspoon ground cinnamon

Do you want the taste of a pork roast, but don't want to spend two or more hours waiting for it? Here's a tender and juicy alternative with the added bonus of moist sweet potatoes and a cinnamon-scented sweet mustard to serve alongside.

1. To make the pork roast: Select Browning/Sauté on the pressure cooker. When the pot is hot, add the canola oil. Tilt the pot to coat the bottom lightly. Add half of the pork and cook for 3 minutes and then turn and cook for 3 minutes longer. Transfer to a plate. Repeat with the remaining pork.

2. Return the reserved pork to the pressure cooker pot and add the water, onion, sage, paprika, garlic powder, and pepper. Lock the lid in place and close the seal valve. Press the Cancel button and reset to Manual for 50 minutes.

3. When the cook time ends, use a quick pressure release.

4. When the valve drops, remove the lid carefully. Check the doneness of the pork roast. Remove the pork with a slotted spoon and place on a platter; cover to keep warm. Add the sweet potatoes to the onion mixture in the pot. Lock the lid in place and close the seal valve. Press the Cancel button and reset to Manual for 4 minutes.

▸ NUTRITION FACTS

Amount Per Serving

Calories	340
Calories from Fat	130

		% Daily Value
Total Fat	14 g	22%
Saturated Fat	5 g	25%
Trans Fat	0 g	
Cholesterol	70 mg	23%
Sodium	430 mg	18%
Total Carbohydrate	33 g	11%
Dietary Fiber	4 g	16%
Sugars	12 g	
Protein	20 g	

Vitamin A		320%
Vitamin C		8%
Calcium		6%
Iron		10%
Magnesium	47.34 mg	
Potassium	652.70 mg	

5. To make the sauce: Combine the sauce ingredients in a small bowl and set aside.

6. When the cook time ends, use a quick pressure release.

7. When the valve drops, remove the lid carefully. Remove the potatoes with a slotted spoon and place alongside the pork and then sprinkle evenly with the salt and drizzle the mustard sauce over all.

▸ **SERVES 8; 3 ounces (85 g) pork, ³/₄ cup (170 g) cooked vegetables, and 1 tablespoon (15 ml) sauce per serving**

Swedish Meatballs and Pineapple on Butternut Spirals

12 ounces (340 g) 93% lean ground turkey

½ cup (40 g) quick-cooking oats

½ cup (50 g) finely chopped green onion (green and white parts)

2 eggs, beaten

1 teaspoon grated fresh ginger

1 teaspoon ground cumin

¼ teaspoon crushed red pepper flakes

½ teaspoon salt, divided

½ cup (120 ml) water

1 can (8 ounces [225 g]) pineapple tidbits in their own juice

1 package (12 ounces [340 g]) frozen butternut squash spirals

2 teaspoons reduced-sodium soy sauce

2 teaspoons honey

¼ cup (4 g) chopped fresh cilantro

To keep your meatballs the same size without pulling out the ruler, simply divide the turkey mixture into four sections and make six meatballs out of each section.

1. Combine the ground turkey, oats, green onion, eggs, ginger, cumin, red pepper flakes, and ¼ teaspoon of the salt in a medium bowl. Shape into 24 small balls, about 1 inch (2.5 cm) each.

2. Select Browning/Sauté on the pressure cooker. When the pot is hot, coat it with cooking spray. Add the meatballs in a single layer; it will be snug. Cook for 3 minutes without turning.

3. Pour the water into the pot over the meatballs. Spoon the pineapple and its juices over all. Do NOT stir. Lock the lid in place and close the seal valve. Press the Cancel button, then reset to Manual for 4 minutes.

Amount Per Serving

Calories	300	
Calories from Fat	90	

		% Daily Value
Total Fat	10 g	15%
Saturated Fat	2.5 g	13%
Trans Fat	0 g	
Cholesterol	155 mg	52%
Sodium	490 mg	20%
Total Carbohydrate	31 g	10%
Dietary Fiber	3 g	12%
Sugars	13 g	
Protein	23 g	

Vitamin A		90%
Vitamin C		25%
Calcium		8%
Iron		20%
Magnesium	33.32 mg	
Potassium	509.76 mg	

4. Meanwhile, cook the butternut squash spirals according to the package directions. Transfer to a platter and cover to keep warm.

5. When the cook time ends, use a quick pressure release.

6. When the valve drops, carefully remove the lid. Check the meatballs for doneness. Remove the meatballs and pineapple with a slotted spoon and place over the squash spirals. Drizzle the soy sauce and honey over the meatballs. Sprinkle with the remaining 1/4 teaspoon salt and the cilantro.

▸ **SERVES 4; 1 cup (177 g) meatball mixture and 3/4 cup (85 g) squash per serving**

Smothered Round Steak with Portobello Mushrooms

1 tablespoon (15 ml) canola oil

1 pound (455 g) boneless bottom round steak, trimmed and cut into 4 pieces

½ teaspoon black pepper

8 ounces (225 g) sliced baby portobello mushrooms

1 cup (160 g) thinly sliced onion

¾ cup (175 ml) water

1 tablespoon (15 ml) Worcestershire sauce

1 tablespoon (16 g) tomato paste

2 teaspoons sodium-free granulated beef bouillon

1 teaspoon dried oregano

½ teaspoon salt

2 tablespoons (8 g) chopped fresh parsley

This is even better the next day, so why not make two pressure cooker meals tonight and know that one will be waiting for you the next night . . . ready when you are!

1. Press Browning/Sauté on the pressure cooker. When the pot is hot, add the canola oil and tilt the pot to coat the bottom lightly. Add the beef and cook for 3 minutes. Turn and sprinkle with the pepper.

2. Top with the mushrooms, onion, water, Worcestershire sauce, tomato paste, beef bouillon granules, and oregano. Lock the lid in place and close the seal valve. Press the Cancel button and reset to Manual for 18 minutes.

3. When the cook time ends, use a 10-minute natural pressure release, then a quick pressure release.

Amount Per Serving

Calories	230
Calories from Fat	90

		% Daily Value
Total Fat	10 g	15%
Saturated Fat	2.5 g	13%
Trans Fat	0 g	
Cholesterol	70 mg	23%
Sodium	420 mg	18%
Total Carbohydrate	8 g	3%
Dietary Fiber	2 g	8%
Sugars	4 g	
Protein	26 g	

Vitamin A		4%
Vitamin C		10%
Calcium		2%
Iron		20%
Magnesium	38.95 mg	
Potassium	740.46 mg	

4. When the valve drops, carefully remove the lid. Check the steaks for doneness. Remove the beef with a slotted spoon and set aside.

5. Press the Cancel button and reset to Browning/Sauté. Bring the liquid in the pot to a boil and cook for 3 minutes, or until reduced to 2 cups (475 ml). Stir in the salt. Spoon the mushroom sauce over the beef and sprinkle with the parsley.

▸ **SERVES 4; 3 ounces (85 g) beef and ½ cup (115 g) mushroom mixture per serving**

7

Fruits and Desserts

Rustic Cinnamon Stick Raspberry Applesauce

2½ pounds (1.1 kg) apples, such as Jonathan or McIntosh, cut into 1-inch (2.5 cm) chunks

1 package (12 ounces [340 g]) frozen raspberries

¾ cup (175 ml) cherry pomegranate juice

1 cinnamon stick

⅛ teaspoon ground allspice

⅛ teaspoon salt

⅓ cup (75 g) packed brown sugar

¼ teaspoon almond extract

No need to peel the apples; it just adds more fiber and texture. Adding the almond extract gives the dish more of a cherry flavor. This makes a lot, so just cover and refrigerate. It gets better and better from one day to the next. This applesauce has a refrigerated shelf life of 10 days.

1. Combine the apples, raspberries, juice, cinnamon stick, allspice, and salt in the pressure cooker pot. Lock the lid in place, close the seal valve, and select Manual for 8 minutes.

2. When the cook time ends, use a quick pressure release.

> **Cook's Note:**
> The applesauce will thicken as it cools. It's even better the next day.

Amount Per Serving

		% Daily Value
Calories	70	
Calories from Fat	0	
		% Daily Value
Total Fat	0 g	
Saturated Fat	0 g	
Trans Fat	0 g	
Cholesterol	0 mg	
Sodium	25 mg	1%
Total Carbohydrate	19 g	6%
Dietary Fiber	2 g	8%
Sugars	15 g	
Protein	0 g	
Vitamin A		0%
Vitamin C		10%
Calcium		2%
Iron		2%
Magnesium	3.27 mg	
Potassium	103.25 mg	

3. When the valve drops, carefully remove the lid. Stir in the brown sugar and almond extract. Stir to break up some of the apples. Let stand for 10 minutes to allow the flavors to blend. Remove the cinnamon stick. Refrigerate until ready to serve.

► **SERVES 12; 1/2 cup (125 g) per serving**

Jump-Out-of-Their-Skins Stuffed Apples

4 red apples (8 ounces ([225 g] each),
  such as Honeycrisp or Gala

1 tablespoon (14 g) light butter
  with canola oil

1 tablespoon (20 g) honey

½ teaspoon ground cinnamon, divided

½ teaspoon vanilla butter and nut flavoring
  or 1 teaspoon vanilla extract

⅛ teaspoon salt

1½ ounces (42 g) finely chopped pecans

1 cup (235 ml) water

These are so much fun to serve—the peels literally pull away from the apples when cooked. But, if you are not a fan of that version, simply choose another variety of apple, such as Red Delicious or Granny Smith, for the skin to stay intact.

1. Core the apples by cutting a slice from the stem end of the apple. Using an apple corer, melon baller, or small teaspoon, remove the apple core, leaving the base intact so it can hold the filling.

2. Combine the butter, honey, ¼ teaspoon of the cinnamon, flavoring, and salt in a small bowl and set aside.

3. Press Browning/Sauté on the pressure cooker. When the pot is hot, add the pecans and cook for 2 minutes or until beginning to lightly brown, stirring frequently. Add the pecans to the honey mixture in the bowl and stir until well blended. Spoon equal amounts of the pecan mixture into each cavity and sprinkle with the remaining ¼ teaspoon cinnamon.

Cook's Note:
You can find vanilla butter and nut flavoring next to the vanilla extract in the spice/baking aisle. It gives a butterscotch flavor to dishes without adding the fat and calories.

Amount Per Serving

Calories	220	
Calories from Fat	80	
		% Daily Value
Total Fat	9 g	14%
Saturated Fat	1 g	5%
Trans Fat	0 g	
Cholesterol	0 mg	
Sodium	95 mg	4%
Total Carbohydrate	33 g	11%
Dietary Fiber	6 g	24%
Sugars	25 g	
Protein	2 g	
Vitamin A		4%
Vitamin C		0%
Calcium		2%
Iron		2%
Magnesium	22.96 mg	
Potassium	261.33 mg	

4. Place 1 cup (235 ml) water in the pressure cooker pot and set a trivet in the pot. Place the apples, cut-side up, on the trivet. Lock the lid in place and close the seal valve. Press the Cancel button and then reset to Manual for 8 minutes.

5. When the cook time ends, use a quick pressure release.

6. When the valve drops, carefully remove the lid. Divide the apples among 4 dessert bowls.

▸ **SERVES 4; 1 apple (184 g) per serving**

Apple-Cherry Bowls with Ginger Crumb Topping

TOPPING:

8 gingersnaps, coarsely crumbled

1½ ounces (42 g) finely chopped walnuts

½ teaspoon ground cinnamon

APPLE-CHERRY BOWLS:

1 cup (235 ml) plus 1 tablespoon (15 ml) water, divided

3 cups (375 g) chopped apples

¼ cup (40 g) dried cherries

1½ teaspoons cornstarch

2 tablespoons (30 g) dark brown sugar

1 tablespoon (14 g) light butter with canola oil

½ teaspoon almond extract

This is the taste of autumn in a bowl: tender, warm, buttery, spiced chunks of apple topped with a quick crumble of gingersnaps, walnuts, and cinnamon.

1. To make the topping: Select Browning/Sauté on the pressure cooker. When the pot is hot, add the cookie crumbled gingersnaps, walnuts, and cinnamon. Cook for 5 minutes, stirring frequently. Transfer the topping to a plate and set aside.

2. To make the apple-cherry bowls: In the pressure cooker pot, combine 1 cup (235 ml) of the water and the apples, making sure the apples are covered with the water. Top with the cherries. Do NOT stir. Lock the lid in place and close the seal valve. Press the Cancel button, then reset to Manual for 3 minutes.

3. When the cook time ends, use a quick pressure release.

NUTRITION FACTS

Amount Per Serving

Calories	230	
Calories from Fat	80	
		% Daily Value
Total Fat	9 g	14%
Saturated Fat	1.5 g	8%
Trans Fat	0 g	
Cholesterol	0 mg	
Sodium	95 mg	4%
Total Carbohydrate	38 g	13%
Dietary Fiber	3 g	12%
Sugars	24 g	
Protein	3 g	
Vitamin A		8%
Vitamin C		10%
Calcium		4%
Iron		8%
Magnesium	29.56 mg	
Potassium	235.38 mg	

4. When the valve drops, carefully remove the lid. Press the Cancel button. Select Browning/Sauté.

5. In a small bowl, whisk the remaining 1 tablespoon (15 ml) water and the cornstarch until the cornstarch dissolves. Stir the cornstarch mixture into the fruit mixture along with the brown sugar. Bring to a boil. Boil for 1 minute, stirring constantly. Turn off the pressure cooker. Stir in the butter and almond extract.

6. Divide the fruit mixture among four shallow bowls or a casserole dish. Top with the crumbled gingersnap mixture and let stand for 15 minutes to allow the flavors to blend.

▸ **SERVES 4; 2/3 cup (142 g) apple mixture and 1/4 cup (28 g) topping per serving**

Soupy "Cookie Dough" Berry Bowls

4 cups (748 g) frozen mixed berries
1 tablespoon (13 g) sugar
½ to 1 teaspoon almond extract
1 package (9 ounces [255 g])
  yellow cake mix
2 tablespoons (28 ml) canola oil
⅛ teaspoon ground cinnamon
1 cup (235 ml) water

This is fun to serve right away while it's very soupy or after it's been refrigerated for a few hours for a thicker consistency. Serve as is for a "cookie dough" taste or for a browner topping, run under the broiler for 1 to 2 minutes; just watch very closely to avoid burning the topping. Either way, the kid in you will definitely be delighted.

1. Combine the frozen berries, sugar, and almond extract in a medium mixing bowl. Toss until well blended.

2. Coat a 1½-quart (1.4 L) round baking dish or oven-safe bowl with cooking spray. Spread the berry mixture in the dish.

3. Place the cake mix in the bowl (the bowl used for mixing berries) and drizzle with the canola oil. Using a spoon, lightly toss the cake and oil to a crumb texture and sprinkle evenly over the fruit. Sprinkle evenly with the cinnamon.

4. Place 1 cup (235 ml) water in the pressure cooker pot and set a trivet in the pot. Wrap the entire pan with aluminum foil. Make a foil sling by folding a 20-inch (51 cm)-long piece of foil in half lengthwise. Place the pan in the center of the sling and lower the pan onto the trivet. Fold down the excess foil from the sling to allow the lid to close properly. (Note: The pan will fit snuggly in the pressure cooker pot.)

5. Lock the lid in place and close the seal valve. Press the Manual button for 30 minutes.

6. When the cook time ends, use a quick pressure release.

7. When the valve drops, carefully remove the lid. Remove the pan using the foil sling. Remove the foil and let stand for 10 minutes. Serve warm or at room temperature in dessert bowls.

▸ **SERVES 8; ½ cup (115 g) per serving**

Hot and Gooey Chocolate Bowls

1/3 cup (42 g) all-purpose flour

1/4 cup (20 g) quick-cooking oats

1/4 cup (20 g) cocoa powder

1 1/2 teaspoons instant coffee granules

3/4 teaspoon baking powder

1/8 teaspoon salt

3 tablespoons (36 g) sugar

1 egg

2 tablespoons (28 ml) canola oil, divided

1 teaspoon vanilla extract

1 cup (235 ml) water

2 squares (1 ounce [28 g] each) 70% dark chocolate, chopped

1 1/2 cups (368 g) vanilla frozen yogurt

This is definitely a chocolate lover's dream. Super moist brownie bowls are topped with frozen yogurt and swimming in pure chocolate sauce.

1. Combine the flour, oats, cocoa, coffee granules, baking powder, and salt in a medium bowl. Stir until well blended.

2. Combine the sugar, egg, 5 teaspoons (25 ml) canola oil, and the vanilla extract in a separate bowl. Stir until well blended.

3. Add the sugar mixture to the flour mixture and stir until just blended.

4. Coat six 6-ounce (170 g) ramekins or custard cups with cooking spray. Divide the mixture among the ramekins. (There will be a scant 2 tablespoons [28 ml] in each ramekin.) Wrap each entirely with foil.

5. Place 1 cup (235 ml) of water in the pressure cooker pot and set a trivet in the pot. Place 3 ramekins on the trivet and top with remaining 3 ramekins. Lock the lid in place, close the seal valve, and select Manual for 4 minutes.

Amount Per Serving

Calories	220	
Calories from Fat	90	
		% Daily Value
Total Fat	10 g	15%
Saturated Fat	3 g	15%
Trans Fat	0 g	
Cholesterol	30 mg	10%
Sodium	160 mg	7%
Total Carbohydrate	30 g	10%
Dietary Fiber	2 g	8%
Sugars	19 g	
Protein	6 g	
Vitamin A		0%
Vitamin C		0%
Calcium		10%
Iron		8%
Magnesium	9.92 mg	
Potassium	195.99 mg	

6. When the cook time ends, use a quick pressure release.

7. When the valve drops, carefully remove the lid. Remove the ramekins from the pressure cooker and let stand for 5 minutes. Carefully remove the foil.

8. Combine the chocolate and remaining 1 teaspoon (5 ml) canola oil in a small microwave-safe bowl and cook for 30 to 45 seconds or until melted. Stir until smooth.

9. Top each serving with 1/4 cup (60 g) of the frozen yogurt and drizzle with 1 tablespoon (15 ml) chocolate sauce.

▶ **SERVES 6; About 1/3 cup (85 g) base, 1/4 cup (61 g) frozen yogurt and 1 tablespoon (15 ml) sauce per serving**

Nut-Crusted Cheesecake Tart with Vanilla Berries

CRUST:

½ cup (55 g) chopped pecans

3 full sheets graham crackers, crushed

2 tablespoons (28 g) light butter
   with canola oil

FILLING:

12 ounces (340 g) reduced-fat
   cream cheese

¾ cup (173 g) nonfat plain Greek yogurt

⅓ cup (67 g) sugar

2 teaspoons flour

1 teaspoon vanilla extract

4 egg whites

1 cup (235 ml) water

TOPPING:

2 cups (290 g) fresh or (310 g) frozen,
   thawed blueberries

2 teaspoons sugar

1 teaspoon vanilla extract

This rich and creamy cheesecake tart has a graham cracker–pecan base and is served piled high with lightly sweetened blueberries and a touch of vanilla.

1. To make the crust: Coat an 8-inch (20 cm) nonstick springform pan with cooking spray and set aside.

2. Press Browning/Sauté on the pressure cooker. When the pot is hot, add the pecans and cook for 4 minutes, or until beginning to lightly brown, stirring frequently. Transfer to a cutting board and finely chop the pecans. Add to a bowl, add the graham cracker crumbs and butter, and mix with a fork to blend. Press into the bottom of the pan.

3. To make the filling: In a blender, combine the cream cheese, yogurt, sugar, flour, vanilla extract, and egg whites. Purée the ingredients until blended. Pour the cheesecake mixture over the prepared crust.

► NUTRITION FACTS

Amount Per Serving

Calories	260	
Calories from Fat	120	

		% Daily Value
Total Fat	13 g	20%
Saturated Fat	5 g	25%
Trans Fat	0 g	
Cholesterol	20 mg	7%
Sodium	310 mg	13%
Total Carbohydrate	27 g	9%
Dietary Fiber	2 g	8%
Sugars	19 g	
Protein	9 g	

Vitamin A		15%
Vitamin C		6%
Calcium		15%
Iron		4%
Magnesium	16.54 mg	
Potassium	176.45 mg	

4. Place 1 cup (235 ml) water in the pressure cooker pot and set a trivet in the pot. Wrap the entire pan with aluminum foil. Make a foil sling by folding a 20-inch (50 cm)-long piece of foil in half lengthwise. Place the pan in the center of the sling and lower the pan onto the trivet. Fold down the excess foil from the sling to allow the lid to close properly. (Note: The pan will fit snuggly in the pressure cooker pot.) Lock the lid in place and close the seal valve. Press the Manual button for 23 minutes.

5. When the cook time ends, use a natural pressure release.

6. When the valve drops, carefully remove the lid. Let the cheesecake rest for 5 minutes in the pressure cooker pot. Use the foil sling to remove the cheesecake from the pot and place it on a wire rack to cool for 1 hour. Cover and refrigerate overnight or for at least 8 hours before serving.

7. To make the topping: Combine the topping ingredients in a medium bowl and refrigerate until needed.

8. Run a knife around the outer edges before removing the sides of the pan. Cut the cheesecake into 8 wedges. Top with the berry mixture.

► **SERVES 8; ⅛ cake and ¼ cup (36 g) berries per serving**

Banana Walnut Snack Cake

2 cups (475 ml) water, divided

1 package (9 ounces [255 g])
 yellow cake mix

½ cup (40 g) quick-cooking oats

1½ teaspoons ground cinnamon

½ teaspoon ground nutmeg

2 ripe medium bananas (about 1⅓ cups
 [300 g] total), mashed

2 tablespoons (28 ml) canola oil

1 egg

1 teaspoon vanilla butter and nut flavoring,
 or 1 teaspoon vanilla extract

4 ounces (115 g) chopped walnuts

This dense, heady cake can be served for dessert, a snack, or breakfast. It's loaded with walnuts, rich banana flavors, and protein.

1. Place 1½ cups (355 ml) the water and a trivet in the pressure cooker pot.

2. Combine the cake mix, oats, cinnamon, and nutmeg in a medium bowl and stir until well blended. Add the remaining ½ cup (120 ml) water, mashed bananas, canola oil, egg, flavoring, and walnuts and stir until just blended.

3. Lightly coat an 8-inch (20 cm) nonstick springform pan with cooking spray. Fill with the batter. Lay a paper towel across the pan, being careful not to let the paper towel touch the batter.

4. Wrap the entire pan with aluminum foil. Make a foil sling by folding a 20-inch (50 cm)-long piece of foil in half lengthwise. Place the pan in the center of the sling and lower the pan onto the trivet. Fold down the excess foil from the sling to allow the lid to close properly. (Note: The pan will fit snuggly in the pressure cooker pot.) Lock the lid in place and close the seal valve. Press the Manual button for 25 minutes.

Amount Per Serving

Calories	270	
Calories from Fat	120	
		% Daily Value
Total Fat	13 g	20%
Saturated Fat	1.5 g	8%
Trans Fat	0 g	
Cholesterol	20 mg	7%
Sodium	220 mg	9%
Total Carbohydrate	35 g	12%
Dietary Fiber	2 g	8%
Sugars	16 g	
Protein	5 g	
Vitamin A		0%
Vitamin C		4%
Calcium		8%
Iron		8%
Magnesium	30.55 mg	
Potassium	189.71 mg	

5. When the cook time ends, use a 10-minute natural pressure release, then a quick pressure release.

6. When the valve drops, carefully remove the lid. Remove the pan from pressure cooker using the sling. Remove the foil, place the pan on a wire rack, and let stand for 30 minutes before removing the sides. The cake will continue to cook as it cools.

7. Run a knife around the outer edges before removing the sides of the pan.

▸ **SERVES 9; 1/9 cake per serving**

Dark Cherry Flan with Dark Chocolate Shavings

1 cup plus 2 tablespoons (263 ml) fat-free evaporated milk

3 tablespoons (45 g) brown sugar

2 eggs

1½ teaspoons vanilla extract

⅛ teaspoon salt

1 cup (235 ml) water

2 squares (1 ounce [28 g] each) 70% dark chocolate, shaved

1⅓ cups (207 g) fresh or frozen, thawed pitted sweet cherries

Wrapping each custard dish entirely with foil prevents any water or steam from getting into the egg mixture. Use tongs or a clean cloth to remove each dish easily and safely when finished cooking. To shave the chocolate, use a vegetable peeler to make pretty curls.

1. In a medium bowl, whisk together the evaporated milk, brown sugar, eggs, vanilla extract, and salt.

2. Coat four 6-ounce (170 g) ramekins or custard cups with cooking spray. Divide the egg mixture among the ramekins. Wrap each entirely with foil.

3. Place 1 cup (235 ml) water in the pressure cooker pot and set a trivet in the pot. Place 3 ramekins on the trivet and top with the remaining ramekin. Lock the lid in place, close the seal valve, and select Manual for 10 minutes.

4. When the cook time ends, use a natural pressure release for 10 minutes, then a quick pressure release.

Amount Per Serving

Calories	220	
Calories from Fat	70	
		% Daily Value
Total Fat	8 g	12%
Saturated Fat	4 g	20%
Trans Fat	0 g	
Cholesterol	95 mg	32%
Sodium	120 mg	5%
Total Carbohydrate	31 g	10%
Dietary Fiber	2 g	8%
Sugars	25 g	
Protein	10 g	
Vitamin A		10%
Vitamin C		6%
Calcium		25%
Iron		10%
Magnesium	22.99 mg	
Potassium	398.21 mg	

5. When the valve drops, carefully remove the lid. Remove the ramekins from the pressure cooker, place on a cooling rack, and carefully remove the foil. Let cool completely. Cover and refrigerate until ready to serve.

6. When ready to serve, invert the ramekins onto 4 dessert plates and spoon equal amounts of the chocolate shavings and the cherries over each serving.

▶ **SERVES 4; 1 (85 g) flan, ½ ounce (15 g) chocolate, and ⅓ cup (52 g) cherries per serving**

Coconut Rice Pudding with Pineapple

1 cup (190 g) brown rice, rinsed and drained

1⅓ cups (315 ml) water

1 can (13.5 ounces [370 ml]) light coconut milk

⅓ cup (67 g) sugar

¼ teaspoon salt

1½ cups (233 g) chopped fresh pineapple

Serving the rice pudding as soon as it's made is my favorite way (and the coconut flavor is more pronounced), but it's delicious served hot or cold— it's your choice.

1. Combine the rice and water in the pressure cooker pot. Lock the lid in place, close the seal valve, and select Manual for 22 minutes.

2. When the cook time ends, use a natural pressure release for 10 minutes, then a quick pressure release.

3. When the valve drops, carefully remove the lid. Stir in the coconut milk, sugar, and salt.

▸ **NUTRITION FACTS**

Amount Per Serving

Calories	220	
Calories from Fat	45	
		% Daily Value
Total Fat	5 g	8%
Saturated Fat	3.5 g	18%
Trans Fat	0 g	
Cholesterol	0 mg	
Sodium	115 mg	5%
Total Carbohydrate	42 g	14%
Dietary Fiber	2 g	8%
Sugars	16 g	
Protein	4 g	
Vitamin A		0%
Vitamin C		35%
Calcium		2%
Iron		4%
Magnesium	49.37 mg	
Potassium	89.62 mg	

4. Press the Cancel button. Select Browning/Sauté. Bring to a boil and boil for 5 minutes or until thickened slightly, stirring frequently.

5. Spoon into bowls and top with the pineapple.

▸ **SERVES 6; ½ cup (151 g) rice mixture plus ¼ cup (39 g) pineapple per serving**

Glazed Almond-Cranberry Bread Pudding

1/3 cup (40 g) confectioner's sugar

1 cup (235 ml) plus 1 tablespoon (15 ml) 2% milk, divided

3 teaspoons vanilla extract, divided

4 ounces (115 g) slivered almonds

4 eggs

2 tablespoons (26 g) granulated sugar

2 teaspoons ground cinnamon

1 teaspoon baking powder

8 ounces (225 g) multigrain Italian bread, cubed

3/4 cup (90 g) dried cranberries or (120 g) cherries

2 cups (475 ml) water

This is a great way to use up day-old or stale bread. Just be sure you tear or cut the bread into uniform pieces so it will absorb the egg mixture evenly. Using a multigrain bread will provide fiber and texture to the overall dish. Toasting the almonds initially will provide a deep nuttiness, too.

1. Stir together the confectioner's sugar, 1 tablespoon (15 ml) of the milk, and 1 teaspoon of the vanilla extract in a small bowl until the sugar has dissolved. Refrigerate until needed.

2. Press Browning/Sauté on the pressure cooker. When the pot is hot, add the almonds and cook for 5 minutes or until beginning to lightly brown, stirring frequently. Transfer to a plate and set aside.

3. In a bowl, combine the remaining 1 cup (235 ml) milk, eggs, granulated sugar, cinnamon, baking powder, and remaining 2 teaspoons vanilla. Whisk until well blended. Fold in the bread cubes and toss until the egg mixture is evenly absorbed.

4. Coat an 8-inch (20 cm) nonstick springform pan with cooking spray. Place the bread mixture in the pan. Sprinkle evenly with the dried cranberries or cherries and top with the almonds. Wrap the entire pan with aluminum foil.

Amount Per Serving

Calories	260	
Calories from Fat	100	

		% Daily Value
Total Fat	11 g	17%
Saturated Fat	1.5 g	8%
Trans Fat	0 g	
Cholesterol	95 mg	32%
Sodium	220 mg	9%
Total Carbohydrate	34 g	11%
Dietary Fiber	6 g	24%
Sugars	19 g	
Protein	11 g	

Vitamin A		4%
Vitamin C		0%
Calcium		15%
Iron		10%
Magnesium	45.32 mg	
Potassium	187.36 mg	

5. Place 2 cups (475 ml) water in the pressure cooker pot and set a trivet in the pot. Make a foil sling by folding a 20-inch (50 cm)-long piece of foil in half lengthwise. Place the pan in the center of the sling and lower the pan onto the trivet. Fold down the excess foil from the sling to allow the lid to close properly. (Note: The pan will fit snuggly in the pressure cooker pot.) Lock the lid in place and close the seal valve. Press the Manual button for 25 minutes.

6. When the cook time ends, use a 10-minute natural pressure release, then a quick pressure release.

7. When the valve drops, carefully remove the lid. Remove the pan from the pot using the foil sling. Remove the foil and then place the pan on a wire rack. Drizzle with the reserved sugar mixture and let stand for 15 minutes. It will continue to cook as it cools.

8. Run a knife around the outer edges before removing the sides of the pan.

▶ **SERVES 8; 3½ ounce (100 g) piece per serving**

ACKNOWLEDGMENTS

To Dan Rosenberg, my editorial director. Thanks for believing in me again and again, Sir!

To John Gettings, my managing editor. Your "fine-tuning" and "quick to respond" ways are greatly, GREATLY appreciated!

To Nyle Vialet, my editorial project manager. You "explained" for me, you worked with me, you were right there for …all of us!

To Melanie McKibbin, my office manager. Keep coming …keep coming and keep the calm.

To Sylvia Vollmer, my right hand in the kitchen. It doesn't matter what time of the day or night you're needed . . . you'll figure out a way to be there … and happily!

ABOUT THE AUTHOR

Nancy S. Hughes is a nationally recognized bestselling author and author-itative food consultant. She has written 21 nationally published cookbooks, including her latest book *Thinner In An Instant Cookbook* with Harvard Common Press. She has also developed recipes for 60 additional cookbooks with over 7,500 published recipes to her credit. Nancy writes for major health organizations (associated with heart, diabetes, and cancer), lifestyle magazines, food companies, and food councils throughout the United States and Canada.

For more information visit her website: www.nancyshughes.com

INDEX

ALSO AVAILABLE

Thinner in an Instant Revised and Expanded Edition
978-1-55832-950-8

Gluten-Free Instant Pot Cookbook
978-1-55832-952-2

Instantly Sweet
978-1-55832-937-9

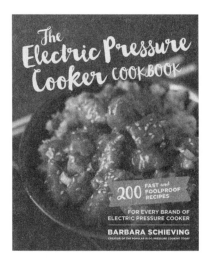

The Electric Pressure Cooker Cookbook
978-1-55832-896-9